No Heroes, No Villains

No Heroes
No Villains

THE STORY OF A
MURDER TRIAL

Steven Phillips

Vintage Books
A Division of Random House, New York

Vintage Books Edition, April 1978

Library of Congress Cataloging in Publication Data

Phillips, Steven.
No heroes, no villains.

1. Richardson, James, 1943-   2. Skagen, John, 1939-1972.
I. Title.
[KF224.R5P54 1978]   345′.73′02523   77-12472
ISBN 0-394-72531-X

Manufactured in the United States of America
9

*To Susan, who shared with me the good
and the bad of both the trial and the book from the start;
this book is dedicated to her with much love*

Author's Note

This book is about the murder of a police officer, and about the trial of a man named James Richardson for the commission of that crime. It is James Richardson's story, and also the story of John Skagen, the man who was killed. It is the story of Pat Skagen, the murdered man's widow, and of George Wieber, a police officer who survived the homicide, but then had to learn to live with its memory.

This book is about William Kunstler, who defended James Richardson at trial. It is about the way he conducted an emotional and politicized defense in an important case.

It is my story as well. I am the assistant district attorney who was assigned to try the Richardson case. It is the story of how I came to be an assistant district attorney in the first place, and of the experiences that prepared me to try a case of this magnitude.

Finally, this account is about an understaffed and underfinanced urban prosecutor's office, struggling with little success to cope with a veritable deluge of street crime. In the broadest sense, I am writing about the criminal justice system in a modern urban setting.

This story is largely without heroes or villains, and those who require such clear-cut divisions will be disappointed. No simple moral may be drawn from my account.

I have written a narrative, not a polemic. However, I have made no effort to hide or disguise my feelings or opinions. I have written from a particular perspective, that of an insider, and I believe that this book has the virtues—and no doubt, the vices—of such a treatment. A less involved or a more neutral observer would probably write a very different book. Nevertheless, I feel that I have an important and exciting story to tell. It is a story that ought to be told.

Acknowledgments

Writing, I have come to learn, is a lonely experience, and one is grateful for good company along the way. I have much to be grateful for.

Michael Meltsner, my friend and former professor, knew I wanted to write this book before I did. His encouragement and guidance have helped me through some hard times, and I am much indebted to him.

My good friend Elaine Romano made many invaluable suggestions, as did Dwight Darcy, Paul Stark and Cecile Grossman, all former colleagues at the district attorney's office. I also owe a great deal to Judge Mary Johnson Lowe for far more than her encouragement and advice.

Gerald Robbie, at Kreindler & Kreindler, read the manuscript with his customary sharp eye and offered many important recommendations. I also received assistance during the preparation of rough drafts from Marka Boyer, Trent Knepper, Mercedes Ludmirski and my secretaries, Mildred Lackey and Nancy Ann Gammino.

Most of all, I owe a deep dept to the many people who figure in this story. Some were adversaries and others were allies, but all of them, without exception, taught me a great deal and made my life richer by their presence. This is especially true of George Wieber and Pat Skagen, two of the most decent people I have ever known. In many ways this book is theirs more than it is mine.

Contents

No Heroes, No Villains

1

The Robbery

No newspaper ever reported the robbery, and it was quickly forgotten. Even the bartender, who for a few terrible moments stared down the barrels of two guns, has little to tell. Marzan's Bar had been robbed before the evening of March 2, 1972, and it has been robbed since. There was nothing unusual about this occasion. Nobody was hurt, not too much money was taken, and in the South Bronx, on the corners of Spofford and Tiffany streets, there is nothing remarkable about an armed robbery.

As nearly as anyone can remember, two black men entered the bar. One was short and wiry, with a medium complexion and an Afro hairstyle; the other was tall and heavy-set, with a dark complexion, close-cropped hair and a moon-shaped face. The shorter man appeared to be the leader. He did the talking.

They walked up to the bar, opposite the cash register, and the short one beckoned to the barkeeper, who was rinsing out used glasses. He put them down and approached the two men. Out came the guns. The short man spoke.

"This is a stickup! Motherfucker, do you hear what I say? This is a stickup!"

The barkeeper put his hands on the counter. He did not panic. "Take what you want. Don't shoot me. I won't do nothin'."

The tall robber went behind the counter and emptied sixty-seven dollars from the cash register. As he was leaving he noticed a woman's purse on a shelf nearby. It belonged to May Elaine Williams, the day barmaid at Marzan's Bar. Almost as an afterthought, he grabbed the purse on his way out of the bar.

The two men fled. From start to finish, the entire robbery had taken no more than forty-five seconds.

The police were called, and ten minutes later a squad car arrived. A patrolman interviewed the witnesses. Later, the barkeeper went down to the 41st Precinct and looked at some mug shots. He was unable to make an identification.

May Elaine Williams had not always worked as a barmaid. A large, buxom, good-looking black woman in her thirties, Mrs. Williams had been employed as a corrections officer at the women's penitentiary at Bedford Hills, New York, until September 1971. She had not been happy at Bedford Hills, and when an illness in her family made the daily trip from her home in the Bronx to the prison in upper Westchester County too burdensome, she quit and took a job near home working at Marzan's Bar. It was a stopgap measure. Soon she began studying at night to become licensed as a practical nurse.

May Elaine Williams was not in the bar at the time of the robbery. She had gone out for a bite to eat. On leaving, she had asked the barkeeper to keep an eye on her purse. By the time she returned, the robbery was over and it was gone.

In the purse at the time of the robbery was a gold correction officer's badge in a blue leather card case which Mrs. Williams had been issued when she first became a corrections officer. She had neglected to return it when she left the Department of Corrections.

On March 4, two days after the robbery, Mrs. Williams received a telegram which read as follows:

MARCH 4, 1972

MRS MAY ELAINE WILLIAMS
621 EAST 170TH STREET
APARTMENT #3 BRONX

PLEASE CALL OR COME TO LINCOLN HOSPITAL
SUNDAY AND COME TO INFORMATION DESK ASK
FOR JAMES RICHARDSON FOR IDENTIFICATION LIN-
COLN HOSPITAL 4:00PM to 12:00PM

Puzzled by this strange message, Mrs. Williams called Lincoln Hospital. She knew no James Richardson and naturally did not connect the telegram with the missing purse or the robbery. When she was unable to reach Richardson, she simply left a message that she had called. One week later he returned her call, and several days after that they met.

Richardson returned to Mrs. Williams her driver's license, her identification papers, and all the contents of her purse except the badge and its carrying case. He explained that he had found these items lying in the gutter on Leggett Avenue several blocks away from Marzan's Bar. When she asked him if he had found a badge along with the papers, he said that he had not. She thanked him for returning the papers, and they parted.

The robbers of Marzan's Bar were never caught.

2

The Subway Station

At 4:50 P.M. John Skagen got off the train. He had finished his day's work an hour earlier and was on his way home.

It had been a tedious day. A Transit Authority patrolman, Skagen had spent the entire morning and afternoon sitting around the Manhattan Criminal Court waiting to give testimony about a pickpocket arrest he had made two weeks earlier. At three-thirty his case was called. His testimony took five minutes and the man he had arrested pleaded guilty.

Skagen, already dressed in civilian clothing, signed out in the sergeant's logbook, took the elevator downstairs, and walked two blocks south to catch the subway. He was eager to get home because he had promised his wife that he would watch their infant son that evening while she joined her girlfriends at a Tupperware party.

It was rush hour and the subway was crowded. Skagen caught the uptown IRT express for the Bronx, rode for about forty-five minutes, and then got off the train at the Hunts Point station. It was his intention to catch the uptown local at Hunts Point. He never made it.

*　　　*　　　*

There were other people at the Hunts Point IRT station that evening besides John Skagen. Calvin Klinger, the token clerk, was two hours into his working day. Robert Jimenez, a sophomore at Morris High School, was helping his mother run the station newsstand. Sylvester Farish, a sixty-one-year-old warehouseman, and Eeda Betancourt, a pretty young secretary, were both on their way home.

James Richardson was there too. A tall black man, with short hair, a dark complexion and a round face, Richardson was wearing dark pants and a waist-length green dashiki. Tucked in his waistband was a nickel-plated, snub-nosed, .32 caliber revolver. Richardson was on his way to begin a day's work as a senior admissions clerk at Lincoln Hospital.

Something about Richardson caught Skagen's attention. Drawing his off-duty revolver and his badge, he approached Richardson yelling, "I'm a cop! Get your hands up! Get against the wall! Get your hands up and get against the wall!"

Richardson complied. Confronted by Skagen's gun, he turned his back and slowly extended his arms until they touched the station walls. Skagen pocketed his badge and stepped forward to frisk Richardson.

Suddenly there was a blur of action and for a split second the two men stood facing each other with guns in their hands. Four shots rang out. Two bullets hit Skagen's shoulder. Another creased Richardson's groin. The fourth ricocheted around the station causing a chip of cement to lodge in Sylvester Farish's forearm.

Richardson fled. Pocketing his gun, he ran through the exit gate and up the stairs toward the street. Skagen, staggered by his injuries, fell backwards, recovered and gave chase. People in the subway station began to scream.

For some weeks the Hunts Point merchants had been upset by the fact that unlicensed street peddlers had been stealing their business and blocking access to their shops. A group of them had gone to the 41st Precinct to complain, and as a result, on the evening of June 28, 1972, when the four-to-midnight tour of the precinct was ready to turn out, the Precinct Conditions officer instructed his men to look out for and ticket any unlicensed peddlers.

At 4:50 P.M. Patrolmen George Wieber and John Jacobsen were standing on the corner of Hunts Point Avenue and Bruckner Boulevard, near the entrance of the Hunts Point IRT subway station. They were writing out a summons for Moises Negron, an unlicensed flower peddler, when the shots were fired. The two officers drew their guns and ran to investigate.

Many people were running and yelling but one man stood out. James Richardson was running up the stairs at full speed shouting, "He's shooting! A crazy man is shooting at me!"

At that instant Skagen arrived at the bottom of the stairs. He raised his gun, aimed, and fired a single shot. Although the shot hit him above the left shoulder blade, Richardson never broke stride and kept right on running.

From the top of the stairs, Patrolman Wieber saw Skagen fire. Wieber aimed his gun down the stairs, pulled the trigger, and kept on firing until his gun was empty and Skagen had fallen.

Richardson ran right into Patrolman Jacobsen's arms. The two men went tumbling out onto Bruckner Boulevard, where Richardson, his adrenaline flowing, recovered first. He drew his gun and pointed it briefly at Jacobsen, then turned and continued his flight.

Jacobsen began to chase Richardson and was joined by Patrolman John Pade. A plainclothes officer, Pade had been across the street with his partner, Patrolman William Rath, when the shooting started. Rath followed into the subway station while Pade went to Jacobsen's assistance. Both of them fired shots at the fugitive as they chased him, but Richardson continued to run.

Patrolman Frank Santiago and Robert Villarubia were in a

patrol car on 163rd Street and Southern Boulevard one block from the subway station when they saw Jacobsen and Pade chasing Richardson. Recognizing the two officers, Santiago, the driver, turned on his lights and siren and took off in pursuit of Richardson.

By now Richardson was running with a limp. He made it across Bruckner Boulevard as far as the fence of the Penn Central Railroad yards. There he threw his gun over the fence into the shrubs that bordered the tracks and ran along the fence.

Santiago, driving the patrol car, cut Richardson off. Gun out, he leaped from the car, threw Richardson against the fence, frisked him and handcuffed him. Jacobsen and Pade arrived seconds later.

At the subway station, Wieber and Rath ran down the stairs to where Skagen lay. He was still conscious. He looked up at them, pulled his badge out of his pocket, and said, "I'm a cop." Then he fainted.

Once the alarm went out, dozens of police officers, ranging in rank from inspector down to patrolman, converged on the Hunts Point subway station. Areas were cordoned off and searched; photographs were taken; witnesses were interviewed and an investigation was launched immediately.

Among the items found on the scene was a blue leather case. Inside the case were identification papers and a social security card belonging to James Richardson. Pinned to the case was a gold correction officer's badge. Investigation revealed that it had been issued to one May Elaine Williams.

3

The Confession

Richardson's injuries were visible. A dark red stain was spreading on the green dashiki over his left shoulder, and his limp had become quite noticeable.

Patrolman Santiago was not certain what Richardson had done. He asked, "Are you shot?"

"Yes, in the groin," Richardson replied.

"Were you shot anywhere else?"

"No."

"It looks to me like you were shot in the shoulder, too."

In the distance they could hear an ambulance siren. Eventually it came into sight, some two blocks away, stuck in the rush-hour traffic. Santiago decided not to wait. He put Richardson in the patrol car, backed it onto the street, and with his siren going, got to Lincoln Hospital in five minutes. As he pulled into the hospital driveway, Santiago heard the first report over the police radio that a police officer had been shot at the Hunts Point subway station. In the emergency room a sergeant told him to stand guard over Richardson.

The emergency room at Lincoln Hospital is chronically overcrowded and understaffed. The evening of June 28, 1972, was no exception to this rule. Once inside, Richardson's handcuffs were removed and he was undressed. An orderly gave him a hospital dressing gown, and he lay down on an examining table in an emergency room cubicle. A nurse came, dressed his wounds and took his pulse and blood pressure. Determining that he was in no immediate danger, she told him to lie quietly and wait for a doctor. As he lay there, Richardson could see the hospital orderlies roll the unconscious John Skagen by on his way to surgery.

Word spread through the hospital that Richardson had been brought in injured. After a few minutes, a friend, Miss Johnson, the hospital property clerk, came to see him. When she asked him what had happened, Richardson looked away. "I think I shot a cop. They say I robbed a change booth."

A doctor did not get around to seeing Richardson until 6:30 P.M. Dr. Roger Smoke, one of the surgical house officers at Lincoln Hospital that evening, did not spend much time with him. He found that a bullet had entered the side of Richardson's left shoulder and had lodged under the skin near his shoulder blade. A second bullet had entered high up in Richardson's groin. It had traveled sharply downward, and exited the side of his right thigh. There was no damage to the major blood vessels and nerves around the other wound. There were no other injuries. Smoke directed that Richardson be catheterized, receive intravenous fluids, and prescribed injections of Demerol and Nembutal to ease any pain. Then he left to attend to other patients.

Detective Luis Cruz of the Transit Authority Police Department was doing paper work in his Brooklyn office when a call came in that a police officer had been shot during a token-booth robbery at the Hunts Point station. He set out immediately for the Bronx. En route he learned over the police radio that a suspect had been taken into custody and was at Lincoln Hospital. It took him over an hour to get to the hospital.

Cruz went directly to the emergency room, where he found Patrolman Santiago standing guard. The two policemen stepped into a corner and conferred quietly. Then Cruz turned to Richardson, took out his badge and identified himself. For the first of five times that night, Richardson was advised of his rights.

"You have a right to remain silent and refuse to answer questions. Do you understand?"

"Yes."

"Anything you do say may be used against you in a court of law. Do you understand?"

"Yes."

"You have a right to consult an attorney before speaking to the police and to have an attorney present during any questioning now or in the future. Do you understand?"

"Yes."

"If you cannot afford an attorney, one will be provided for you free of cost. Do you understand?"

"Yes."

"If you do not have an attorney available, you have a right to remain silent until you have an opportunity to consult with one. Do you understand?"

"Yes."

"Now that I have advised you of your rights, are you willing to answer questions without an attorney present?"

"Yes."

The following are Detective Cruz's notes of that statement:

I was on my way to work today at Lincoln Hospital. I went into the Hunts Point Station. I had walked up to the stairway leading to the southbound train and this guy stopped me. We had words which I can't remember and the guy pulled his gun and shield and I pulled mine—a chrome-plated .32 calibre snubnosed revolver. I had my gun tucked inside my pants up front. Then the cop shot me right here (indicating lower right groin) and I shot him. I'm sorry. I hope the cop pulls through.

The statement took only a few minutes and then Cruz set off to tell his superiors what he had learned.

At seven o'clock, Richardson was taken upstairs from the emergency room to Ward 4B, placed in an adjustable hospital bed, was catheterized, and began to receive intravenous fluids.

About ten minutes later Patrolman Santiago decided to question Richardson himself. From memory, he readvised Richardson of his rights. Again Richardson chose to speak.

"Look, I was on my way to work at Lincoln Hospital. I went down into the station when this white guy asked me where I was going. I told him, and I told him who I was. Then I asked him who the hell he was, and he told me he was with the Transit Authority. I said I had lots of friends in the Transit Authority, and we had words. We pulled out our guns and shot each other. I ran up the stairs."

Blondell Gimbell, Richardson's cousin, and his girlfriend, Brenda Wright, had heard that he was hurt and came to see how he was. Richardson asked Miss Gimbell not to tell his mother about what had happened. "I don't want her to worry about my always being in trouble."

"How do you feel?" she asked.

"I'm okay. I hope the guy upstairs pulls through."

"What guy?"

"The cop. I shot him. He shot me and then I shot him."

Detective Richard Gest was "catching" on the evening of June 28, 1972. Assigned to the 8th Homicide-Assault Squad covering the South Bronx, he was responsible for any homicide or serious assault investigations initiated that evening. At 5 P.M. he caught the Hunts Point subway shooting.

Detective Gest went first to the scene of the shooting and began his investigation there. It was not until about eight o'clock that he arrived at Lincoln Hospital to question Richardson.

Gest was unaware of Detective Cruz's earlier questioning, so for the third time that night Richardson was read the catechism of his rights, and for the third time he agreed to talk. Again he repeated the now familiar story of the confrontation in the subway station. Then a new question was asked, "Why did the white man pick you, out of all the other people in the station?"

"He probably saw the gun tucked inside my trousers."

"What did you do with the gun?"

"I threw it over the fence before they caught me."

Detective Gest left. He knew that an assistant district attorney would arrive later to take a formal stenographic statement from Richardson, and Gest had a lot to do that night. It would be noon of the following day before he got any sleep.

Something about all of this questioning left Richardson uneasy. He wanted it clearly understood that he had not robbed anybody. Finally, he said, "I want the Spanish detective. I want to set things straight." Someone went to look for Luis Cruz.

It was eight-thirty when Cruz came hurrying back to the ward. He assured Richardson that there was no evidence that a robbery had taken place, and that he was not charged with one. Ever cautious, he readvised Richardson of his rights and again took notes of what Richardson had to say.

I was inside the turnstiles and was going towards the stairway towards the back of the train. I was called by a man, "Hey fella", and he came over and we had words. The man pulled out his gun on me with his shield and I pull out mine from under my dashiki.

The gun was under my dashiki, tucked inside my pants—a chrome-plated .32 snubnosed revolver. The cop fired at me from about six feet away and then I fired my gun at him. I ran up the stairs to the street. I grappled with a big uniformed cop on the street. He sure was a big cop but I broke away from him and ran across Bruckner Boulevard to the southeast corner at Hunts Point Avenue and then turned south. Bullets kept whizzing by my head. They were really trying to do me in. Then I was cut off by a police car, and I went up against the fence of the railroad yard. The cop in the subway shot me in the groin. I don't remember when I was shot in the rear shoulder.

Richardson then complained of pain in his shoulder, and Cruz stopped his questioning.

An assistant district attorney was the last person to question Richardson that night. Michael DuBoff went first to the 41st Precinct, where he questioned Patrolmen Wieber and Jacobsen and conferred with police officials. DuBoff may have been the first to learn that Skagen had been shot by both Richardson and Patrolman Wieber. Then he went to Lincoln Hospital. The following is a transcript of the stenographic statement that was taken by the assistant district attorney:

Q. You have a right to remain silent. You don't have to say anything. Do you understand?
A. Right.
Q. And if you do say something, it could be used against you in a court of law. Do you understand that?
A. Right.
Q. And you have a right to a lawyer.
A. Right. I have one coming.
Q. And if you can't afford an attorney, you can get one free of charge.
A. I think I have an attorney. As a matter of fact, I'll let you know everything tomorrow. Right now I wish they'd either cut this thing or just do something.

Q. What's that, the arm?

A. Yah. I'm pressing on the bullet, and they can't do nothing.

Q. Do you want to tell me what happened from the beginning?

A. I don't know where the beginning was. The officer approached me. Now we know he's an officer. Then he was—he looked like ugh, dingy, run down. He didn't look like no policeman and he said fellow, sounded like fellow. Anyway, he hit a nerve right there. I think if I would approach anybody I would say sir. I know I don't look like a child, but fellow? I turned, and we started passing words. At one time all I saw was a badge and a gun, I mean anybody could flash a badge on you but I think if I was a police officer, I would say police officer and the average person is going to say let me see your number. We didn't even get to that. As a matter of fact, that's when we started passing words, nasty. The next thing I know he hit me here.

Q. Hit you in the groin with what?

A. With his gun.

Q. The gun itself, I mean he fired at you?

A. He shot me here, I'm stunned. It was the first time I was ever shot. Now, I don't remember firing on him, it could have been. Everything happened like in seconds, like in seconds. All I remember is turning and running. I don't know where he fell, if he was hit—nothing.

Q. What happened when you ran?

A. I remember tackling or think I remember tackling with a big giant, he was huge.

Q. A police officer?

A. Right.

Q. In uniform?

A. Yeah he was huge, very huge. He could have easily collared me. Then I ran and that's when the world came to an end. All I felt was the breezes coming around my head. I know it was seven.

Q. Seven shots?

A. I counted seven breezes, there could have been more. It seemed like everyone was aiming at me. I don't know where I got this from.

Q. Meaning the shot in the arm?

A. Right. I could have gotten it upstairs. I could have gotten it in the street. I don't remember.

Q. How about the one in your back?

A. That's what I'm talking about. They knew I had been shot because I'm bleeding, and they continued beating me. They had me against the fence. They said your ass is ours now, all I could see was sticks and feets.

Q. Then what?

A. Then they brought me here slowly, but we got here.

Q. How long do you think it took?

A. Well I believe if they would have had the siren on, I mean like an emergency, from there we could of came straight on down the boulevard, turned right there at the diner on the corner of Southern Boulevard, came up the ramp. They came down Southern Boulevard where all the traffic is, almost stopping for every light.

Q. Let's go back to the train station. Why did the police officer stop you?

A. It's a possibility he seen my gun.

Q. Where did you have your gun?

A. In my navel.

Q. Sticking out of your pants?

A. No.

Q. How was it?

A. In the pants.

Q. Like this?

A. Yeah. Now this is possible, you know.

Q. Sort of tucked in your pants around the front area?

A. Right. But why did he stop me really? Because he looked like ugh. A police officer is supposed to look presentable.

Q. Where were you coming from?

A. I was coming from home, coming here.

Q. Where do you work?

A. Right here.

Q. At Lincoln Hospital?

A. Right. I called them because the old lady hadn't came back yet. I told them I would be about 15 or 20 minutes late I had to take care of the kids this is why I called them to let them know I would be late. So I was coming from the house to here in the subway. Any other time I would take the bus but because I was late I took the subway. It would have been a little quicker than the bus.

Q. Why did you have the gun with you?

A. I been threatened three or four weeks ago.

Q. So you carried a gun?

A. Well, I don't carry it because I never carry it. But I had plans on staying out tonight and this fellow threatened me and the old lady and pulled their guns on her. It was either me and her or them. There was five of them.

Q. Who were these fellows?

A. Her husband and his friends. They filed for divorce, and they were going to Family Court. If he was a man, he would just leave her alone. He threatened her, whipped her, and kicked her in the stomach and his friends were waiting for me one night to come home. She had took them to the 41st. A police car came by and she had the family court warrant. She took them and the friends laid around the house waiting for me.

Q. When did this happen?

A. About three or four weeks ago.

Q. And when did you get the gun?

A. About two days after this happened.

Q. Where did you get the gun? Whose gun is it?

A. I'd rather not say.

Q. What happened to the gun today?

A. This is a good question.

Q. What did you do with it?

A. That's a good question too.

Q. Does that mean you don't want to answer?

A. You could say that.

Q. Anything you don't want to tell me about or say you don't have to.

A. I'm not afraid to speak to you or these fellows here. It was a nightmare. I don't want to go through it again. But the nightmare was being fired at. I could feel the breeze of these bullets going through the air. Everybody was aiming for the head.

Q. Listen, in the subway station who fired first?

A. He did. I know this because I was stunned.

Q. Did you have your gun out when he fired?

A. As a matter of fact, I was more like ignoring him because he looked like ugh. I'm working man going to work and this ugh —I mean the way he was dressed. I never seen a police officer even if he's off duty—he either got a crease in his pants or something but his fellow looked like ugh, and we passed too many words.

Q. What kind of words?

A. They were nasty.

Q. Do you remember any of them?

A. No, not really. I know he did ask me what was my name, where was I going. This is what hit a nerve.

Q. Did you tell him?

A. As a matter of fact this is what hit a nerve because he was giving me the third degree and hadn't presented himself yet.

Q. Did he ask you why you had the gun?

A. Never even got to that.

Q. When did you draw your gun? When did you take it out of your pants?

A. Almost when I was stunned, knowing that I was shot.

Q. Did you have a gold badge?

A. Let me think back to see what I left the house with because I know I have none of it here. I left with a set of keys, a ten dollar bill, a fifty cent Kennedy piece 71, a quarter, and a nickel, and four little candies, handkerchief, cigarettes and my phone book. I've had my wallet stolen a couple of times, so I use my phone book as identification.

Q. How about your driver's license?

A. I don't drive.

Q. Do you have a Social Security card?

A. You know I don't have that. That was in my phone book, my union card, my card like when I get prescriptions, Medicaid card, all prescriptions, I pay seventy-five cents, draft card, picture of the old lady and my phone book with a red rubber band.

Q. You have a draft card like this?

A. Right.

Q. Selective form number 2, selective service registration form.

A. Yeah I had one of those.

Q. What kind of a gun was it?

A. I really couldn't say because I know nothing about guns.

Q. It was loaded, right?

A. It had one thing in it, one bullet in it.

Q. Only one?

A. I don't know.

Q. After you got hit in the groin, did you fire your gun?

A. No I didn't fire at him.

Q. How close were you from him?

A. I know how close he was, it went in one end and came out the other end of me. I got two things here.

Q. And he was the same distance away?

A. I know he was a little further after he hit me, but I'm stunned, I backed up. As a matter of fact, when he shot me, that backed me up.

Q. You weren't thrown up against the wall when he shot you?

A. No I wasn't up against the wall.

Q. Did you have your hands up?

A. No I didn't have my hands up either.

Q. Never had your hands up?

A. No no it happened in an instant. We passed words a little bit and then it happened like that.

Q. Where were you standing when you shot?

A. I really couldn't say how close after he shot me.

Q. Where in the subway were you standing?

A. I was getting ready to pay for the token. I passed the turnstile and he approached me.

Q. Where were you when you actually fired?

A. That's a good question, a damn good question because I don't even know where he was.

Q. Were you near a wall out in the open?

A. Well it seemed like it was me and him, nobody else. The odd part about it was that it was rush hour because I know when I leave to come to work to be here at 4:30 it's packed so I go and get the bus. I don't want to get on no sardine train so I know I was an hour late and rush hour gets heavier. It seemed like it was me and him and nobody else.

Q. Is there anything else you can think of that you left out that you want to add?

A. What are the charges?

Q. That's a good question. I don't know.

A. Well I heard some rumors you know. I just hope three things, that he's all right, his family's all right and my family's all right. These are the only three things I hope. I don't want to say that he was right and I don't want to say I was right. You don't want to say he was wrong or I was wrong. It was just a bad scene all the way around and to know that you're so close to death. I died a thousand times. I don't know if you ever been shot before or even been shot at. There wasn't no gaps because all I could hear was pow, pow, pow. I could just feel the breezes coming by me from the neck coming up to the head part. This is death in itself. If I had to go through that again, I couldn't.

Q. Well, you think you're wrong?

A. Well, like I said, I don't think I was wrong or he was wrong or I was right or he was right. It was just a bad thing from the beginning to end.

Q. Is there anything else you want to add about what happened? Do you think he was trying to take you off?

A. For your sake I'm not going to say yes. I don't want to say yes, it could be possible.

Q. Do you think it was self defense?

A. It could be possible. He shot me first.

Q. Well, you weren't taking anybody off when he came over, right?

A. That's definitely out.

Q. But you had the gun by your navel.

A. Taking him off for what?

Q. You weren't, I know you weren't.

A. Have you all looked at my record? It's not up to par but I'm not getting laid off because of it so to make that statement what you just said take him off.

Q. The statement I made was you weren't.

A. No, no, hell, now, I wasn't taking nobody off.

Q. You think you fired to protect yourself?

A. Well you can say maybe self defense. May I ask a question?

Q. Sure.

A. Do all law enforcement officers in New York have almost the same procedure for presenting themselves to an unknown person. I'm asking you two right here because you're both different branches, do you all present yourselves the same way? Why did he wait to present himself to me. He has to say a little more and do a little more to show that he's a police officer. If he's stopping me or suspicious of me for something, don't hesitate because we had words before, and then I still wouldn't say he was a police officer. I never even seen the badge.

Q. Why did he shoot you?

A. That's what I'd like to know. Why I ask [is] because I thought you supposed to either point your gun at the person or shoot a warning shot in the air or something letting somebody know something was happening. This is what I'm asking. I knew nothing and I don't think he knew nothing because he looked like ugh.

Q. Where do you live?

A. Hunts Point. 710 or 720. Now why I'm saying this is because my mother lives in 720—710 or 720.

Q. What apartment?

A. 4A.

Q. What's your wife's name?

A. Brenda Wright.

Q. And how many kids does she have?

A. Three. We supposed to be expecting one like maybe one month.

Q. One month?

A. No we just got together and figure one month.

The following day Dr. Bruce Herzog removed a bullet from Richardson's shoulder and turned it over to the police.

Richardson recovered quickly and was discharged from Lincoln Hospital on July 9. From there he was taken to the Bronx House of Detention for Men.

4

The Operation

Patrolman Rath carried Skagen up the station stairs in his arms. He flagged down a patrol car, and they set off for Lincoln Hospital, siren screaming. Skagen was slumped in the back seat, unconscious and bleeding heavily. Rath bent over him, pressing his hands over the wounds in a vain attempt to stop the flow of blood. He tried giving Skagen mouth-to-mouth resuscitation. It did no good. Skagen's heart had stopped beating by the time they reached the hospital.

New York City has a number of the finest hospital complexes in the world. There are great university medical centers, staffed with some of the best physicians that can be found anywhere. Important medical research is done in New York City in dozens of different fields. Patients with particularly complicated medical problems, or with rare diseases, are routinely sent to the city to receive special treatment.

Lincoln Hospital, located in the South Bronx, has little if anything to do with any of this kind of medicine. At best,

Lincoln Hospital is a mediocre institution. It is understaffed and underfinanced, and it struggles along under impossible conditions. The entire litany of slum problems—overcrowded tenement housing, violent crime, drug abuse, bad diet, inadequate public sanitation, ignorance, poverty and despair—can be recited to indicate a community health problem that would swamp any hospital.

Lincoln Hospital is no stranger to controversy. In 1970 its buildings were seized by a group of Puerto Rican radicals, who proclaimed the institution a "People's Hospital" and agitated to expel non-Hispanic doctors in favor of Hispanic ones. Youth gang members have roamed the hospital's halls terrorizing both patients and staff, and at one time in April 1972 surgeons performing life-saving procedures on a wounded member of one youth gang actually had to barricade themselves in the operating room to prevent members of a rival gang from "finishing off" a job they had started out on the streets. Anarchy would be a fair characterization of the state of affairs at Lincoln Hospital in the spring of 1972.

In spite of this, there is one area in which Lincoln Hospital is said to excel: emergency surgery. No emergency room in the country receives a more steady diet of gunshot and knife wounds than the emergency room at Lincoln Hospital. As a result, it attracts a large number of talented young surgeons, eager to improve their skills on the hospital's large and varied caseload.

Indeed, Lincoln Hospital's reputation for "combat surgery" is so good that many police officers candidly state that if injured they would rather be taken to its emergency room than to any of the far more prestigious hospitals available. Of course, the same officers are equally unanimous in detesting other aspects of the hospital. It is often said, only half in jest, that the leading cause of death in the South Bronx is "Lincoln-itis."

*　　　　*　　　　*

In any event, the surgical team that went to work on John Skagen was undoubtedly a good one. Right in the emergency room they opened up his chest and began open heart massage. The surgeons noticed no heavy bleeding in the open chest cavity from the two shoulder wounds. Skagen responded to the massage. His heart began to beat. He was still alive.

Skagen was then wheeled up to the operating room and given massive transfusions of blood. The surgeons opened up his belly to examine the damage done by what appeared to be three bullet wounds. His abdominal cavity was filled with blood. The doctors set about repairing the damage. Most of the blood loss came from a tear in the major artery which feeds blood into the lower digestive tract and legs. Skagen's bladder was lacerated, and there was a hole in a loop of his large intestine. The surgeons performed a colostomy and patched up the tear in the major artery and bladder. Then Skagen's heart stopped for the second time.

Many people were at the hospital that night. John Lindsay was there, flanked by aides. Burton Roberts, the district attorney of Bronx County, also came, and all the police brass were there. They received hasty and periodic briefings on the progress of the investigation, but in the final analysis all they could do was wait.

Someone else was there as well. Pat Skagen had been called, and was told that her husband had been shot. She found a neighbor to watch their young son and drove to the hospital. When she arrived she could find no one who could tell her what had happened. Finally she found a police officer who took her to a hallway near the emergency room. There she waited, ignored by everyone.

The surgeons got Skagen's heart going a second time. He was weak. He had lost a tremendous amount of blood, but he was alive, and the damage had been repaired. It looked as if he might pull through after all. Then, at exactly nine o'clock, his heart stopped for a third time. This time the dilation was acute and all efforts at revival were in vain. John Skagen was dead.

The next morning the mayor's office issued the following press release:

Last night the city lost a brave transit patrolman in a tragedy that is still under investigation. Officer John Skagen died in a chain of circumstances that began with his efforts to question a man with a gun. As of this time we can only speculate on the final report. But it is clear that Officer Skagen was, in a sense, the victim of this nation's obsession with handguns. To Officer Skagen's wife and family and friends, I extend the heartfelt sympathies of all New Yorkers, and I pledge a relentless battle for the national control of handguns and an end to violence in this nation.

John V. Lindsay

5

The Gun

Within seconds of Richardson's arrest, Jacobsen, Pade and Villarubia had climbed the fence, and began searching through the undergrowth of the railroad yard. They were winded by their exertions, and far from systematic in their approach. They wandered back and forth, duplicating each other's efforts. Some neighborhood kids also jumped the fence, curious to see what the cops were up to. Nobody bothered to chase them away.

George Wieber arrived at the railroad yard, found his partner, Jacobsen, and said in a dead tone, "I think I shot a cop." The four men stood silently, shaken; then Wieber and Jacobsen returned to their patrol car and left for Lincoln Hospital.

Within an hour the Emergency Services Squad arrived, and the search for the gun began in earnest. A huge area of the train yard was cordoned off, high-intensity lights were set up, and systematically, yard by yard, policemen combed through the underbrush. They worked well into the night, checking and double-checking each area, but they found nothing. Frustrated, they gave up.

Where was the gun? Almost a dozen people had seen Richardson throw it into the railroad yard, Richardson himself had admitted that it was there, and yet an intensive search failed to produce it. The only possible answer, and the conclusion soon reached, was that one of the neighborhood kids must have found it. A team of detectives was assigned to continue the search.

Finding a gun in the 41st Precinct is easy. Guns are as common on the streets of the South Bronx as they once were in Dodge City. But finding a specific gun, especially once the word is out that it "killed a cop," is a different story altogether.

It is difficult for an outsider to grasp the realities of the South Bronx. In a physical sense the Hunts Point area in 1972 compared unfavorably with Berlin in 1945. Bombed-out and abandoned buildings, occupied by drunks and junkies, are commonplace. Filthy, roach-infested, unbelievably overcrowded tenements comprise the remainder of the standing structures. Violence and despair are a way of life in this neighborhood. Even in the prosperous pre-recession days of 1972, the unemployment rate in Hunts Point hovered above 25 percent. It was even higher among the young men of the neighborhood. Those who could find work almost invariably got the most menial and unpleasant jobs that society offered.

In the middle of this neighborhood sits the 41st Precinct. In 1972 the Four-One was easily the busiest precinct in New York City. Charged with the impossible job of maintaining law and order under these conditions are approximately 330 police officers. They are responsible for about 2.5 square miles of territory, containing 60 miles of street and a population of 171,000—broken down at the last census as 98,000 Puerto Rican, 62,000 black and 11,000 designated as "others." Most policemen view assignment to the Four-One in about the same way that German soldiers of World War II viewed combat assignments on the Russian front. Dealing with a world almost completely alien and hostile to his own, a police officer is made to feel that the precinct is a lonely outpost of "civilization." The 41st Precinct is known as Fort Apache. Before 1972 was over, there would be 101 murders in the 41st Precinct and violence would become the number one cause of death for those under thirty in Hunts Point.

Detectives Hank Arana, Juan Caban and Luis Cruz all grew up in areas like Hunts Point. They are street wise. That is, they speak the language of such a neighborhood and are familiar with its values. They are not often "made" as cops, even by the alert rip-off artists and junkies who inhabit their working world. In short, they are good detectives. They were given the unenviable job of trying to recover James Richardson's gun.

They fanned out through the neighborhood, looking up old acquaintances, people they had helped or who had helped them in the past.

"Hey, man, I'm looking for a piece."

"Shit, what you looking for a piece for? You a cop."

"I'm looking for a special piece. The one that was used to kill the cop over at the Hunts Point station. What do you know about it?"

"Nothing."

So it went day after day, until finally Hank Arana came up with a lead. He found a fifteen-year-old named Ralph Lugo who told him that he had been down at the railroad yard when the cops had been searching for Richardson's gun. More important, he had seen one of the neighborhood kids bend down, pick up a shiny object, and put it in his belt. The word was that this kid had found the gun.

"What's the kid's name? Do you know him?"

"No. I've just seen him around sometimes."

"Where does he live?"

"Around Southern Boulevard."

After talking to others Arana was able to identify the youth's name as Raul Bianchi. Arana set out to find him. On July 7 he succeeded in finding Bianchi who was "hanging out" on Southern Boulevard. At first Bianchi was scared and wary when Arana identified himself as a cop, but after being assured that he would not be prosecuted he decided to cooperate.

Bianchi told Arana that he had seen the police hunting for something at the railroad yard and had climbed over the fence to investigate. In the bushes he had found a small silver-colored gun, about five inches long, with the word CLERKE written on its handle. Bianchi pocketed the gun and went home. In the backyard of his apartment building, he had pulled a pin and unloaded the gun. It contained one live round and four spent cartridges. The figure #.32 was stamped on the back of each cartridge. He had thrown them into the litter of the backyard, but he had kept the gun. The following day he had sold it to "an older man" for sixty-five dollars. He used the money to buy a pair of shoes.

Arana did not end his search, but he never found the man who had bought the gun, or if he did, the man did not admit to it. But then again, in Hunts Point, who would?

The search for Richardson's gun was only one element of the investigation that followed John Skagen's death. The rest was far less dramatic, and in the final analysis, far more important. There was no manhunt, and none of the heroics that the public has come to expect in the solution of murder mysteries. Instead there was a careful but routine compilation of data, of old files and physical evidence by police technicians and scientists. The medical examiner performed an autopsy, and ballistics men analyzed the police officers' guns and the bullets that were recovered. Slowly, painstakingly, information was accumulated, and a picture began to emerge.

6

James Richardson

There is a widespread belief that the police have at their disposal voluminous files which contain detailed life histories of every citizen, or at least of anyone with a prior criminal record. The truth is far more prosaic. Government information-retrieval systems are notoriously haphazard and inefficient, and the information contained in the files is usually sketchy, incomplete, unreliable and of little value.

Nevertheless, early in the investigation of the Hunts Point shooting, efforts were made to find out something about James Richardson's background. These efforts were not strenuous, and the focus of the inquiries was to discover any information which might either strengthen the factual case against the defendant, or tie him to some larger criminal enterprise. No one tried to uncover the inner dynamics of Richardson's personality, or explain what might have motivated him on June 28, 1972. These latter questions, undoubtedly the most important that might have been asked, were not important to the police, who frankly were neither equipped nor inclined to act as amateur sociologists or psychiatrists. Consequently, little was revealed about James Richardson, the man, during the police investigation. Neither the police nor the prosecution ever gained much insight into his personality.

Indeed, after that first night at Lincoln Hospital, no law enforcement official would ever be permitted to talk to Richardson directly, and no attempt would be made to interview his friends, relatives or acquaintances. It was assumed that there would be no cooperation or useful information from these sources—only accusations that there had been an attempt to tamper with the defense. Thus, for law enforcement, Richardson would become a phenomenon largely defined by his deeds on the evening of June 28, 1972.

Briefly stated, the information that was available revealed that on June 28, 1972, Richardson was twenty-eight years old, having been born on November 29, 1943, in New York City. His parents appeared to be hard-working, law-abiding citizens, and he had two sisters both younger than himself.

He had been married but was separated from his wife and their two children. Prior to his employment as an admitting clerk at Lincoln Hospital in 1970, his work record had been sporadic.

At the time of his arrest, Richardson was five feet eleven and a half inches tall and weighed a muscular hundred and eighty pounds. Small scars were noted over his left eye and on his left cheek, right ankle and left forearm. His hair was noted as black and his eyes as brown.

He had reached the twelfth grade at Samuel Gompers High School in New York City, but had not graduated. It was also revealed that over the years Richardson had had some minor conflicts with the law. There was a 1967 marijuana conviction in Rochester, New York, leading to a sentence of three years on probation. He had violated the terms of this probation by failing to report to his probation officer. There was a warrant issued for his arrest on the parole violation, and technically on June 28, 1972, he still owed several months in jail on it.

In addition, he had been arrested in Brooklyn in 1970, as a passenger in a stolen car, and had been charged with acting in concert with the driver in the theft. Once out on bail in that case, he had again failed to return to court, and in due course another warrant had been issued for his arrest.

All told, it was not a very serious record. There were no crimes of violence, and only one conviction for the possession of marijuana. He had jumped bail, and was technically a fugitive from justice, although this had hardly prevented the City of New York from hiring him to fill a reasonably responsible position. In the final analysis, given the realities of big-city life, there was nothing extraordinarily bad about James Richardson's background—certainly, nothing that would seem to shed any light on this case.

7

The Autopsy

Skagen's body was taken to the morgue that night. The following morning, in the presence of eight other members of the medical examiner's staff, Dr. Justin Uku, an associate medical examiner, performed an autopsy.

The office of the chief medical examiner of the City of New York is charged by law with the investigation of all violent, accidental, unexplained or otherwise suspicious deaths in the five boroughs. In 1972 approximately eight thousand autopsies were performed in discharge of this responsibility. Homicides, suicides, automobile accidents, drug overdoses and child abuse are all common fare at the medical examiner's office. At any given moment, often around the clock, as many as four or five autopsies may be simultaneously in progress.

To visit the autopsy room of the medical examiner's office can be an unnerving experience. Cadavers lie on cold steel examining tables with their toes tagged for identification, each in a different state of dissection. Some appear quite human; others are only grotesque hollow shells of what were once living individuals. There is a strong smell of disinfectant and the constant sound of running water used to wash away the liquid wastes of the dissection. To watch an autopsy is to see mankind reduced to so much physical matter, to flesh only, with all personality or spirit stripped away. It is a process, and a sight, that takes some getting used to. The end product of an autopsy is a protocol, meticulously listing the medical examiner's findings and certifying a cause of death.

Skagen's autopsy revealed that he had been a well-developed thirty-two-year-old white male. He was six feet one inch tall and weighed a hundred and fifty-four pounds.

Careful note was made of the various scars, incisions, sutures and drains from the previous day's operation. There was a total of eight bullet wounds, caused by five bullets. Five were entry wounds, two were exit wounds and one was a reentry wound. Four bullets were recovered.

The first bullet recovered struck Skagen in the upper right shoulder and traveled from right to left, downward and backward, passing through the shoulder muscles and lodging in the rear of the chest. This bullet was marked S (for Skagen)/$U1$ (for Uku, the examiner in charge).

The second bullet recovered hit Skagen on the side of the left hip and traveled from left to right, downward and forward, until it hit the pelvic bone. Then it deflected upward and lodged against the abdominal wall. This bullet was marked $S/U2$.

The third bullet recovered hit Skagen on the side of the left buttock, and traveled from left to right, downward and forward through the hipbone and a loop of the large intestine. It exited through the right buttock and then reentered and lodged in the outside of the right buttock. This bullet was marked $S/U3$.

The fourth bullet recovered struck Skagen in the front of his left hip and traveled from left to right, downward and backward, tearing the left external iliac artery and the urinary bladder. It lodged in the right buttock. It was labeled $S/U4$.

The fifth bullet struck Skagen in the upper right shoulder where the arm and the shoulder meet and moved from right to left, slightly downward and horizontally through the muscle and soft tissue of the shoulder. It exited from Skagen's back and was not recovered.

Sections of tissue and blood samples were taken and examined for the presence of alcohol or narcotics. These tests proved negative.

All of the recovered bullets were given to the police, and a death certificate was prepared and signed by Dr. Uku. It certified the cause of death as follows:

> BULLET WOUNDS OF SHOULDER, BACK, CHEST, AB-
> DOMEN, EXTERNAL ILIAC ARTERY, BLADDER, PEL-
> VIS AND LOWER EXTREMITIES. HEMOPERITONEUM,
> HOMICIDAL.

8

John Skagen

The autopsy completed, Skagen's body was taken to the Walter B. Cooke Funeral Home, on Westchester Avenue in the Bronx, where a wake was held for three days. Funeral services were held on July 3 at the Holy Family Roman Catholic Church, and on the same day the body was interred at Saint Raymond's Cemetery on East Tremont Avenue.

John Skagen was buried with pomp and ceremony. He was given an inspector's funeral, an honor accorded police officers who are killed in the line of duty. The service was attended by high police officials and other dignitaries, a special honor guard, delegations from other police departments in the New York metropolitan area, representatives from the Patrolmen's Benevolent, the Steuben and the Emerald societies, and a number of friends, colleagues and relatives.

Skagen's police personnel folder was pulled and reviewed by detectives in the possibility that it might contain information shedding some light on his death. But the file was as useless to the police as Richardson's had been.

*   *   *

Jackie Skagen was born in the Bronx on January 15, 1939, the eldest of four children of Charles and Mary Skagen. A high school dropout, he enlisted in the United States Navy and served for almost twelve years, reaching the rank of petty officer and quartermaster first class. While in the service he received a high school equivalency diploma, and on May 22, 1970, he was honorably discharged.

On February 8, 1964, Skagen was married to the former Patricia Muend at Saint Luke's Church in the Bronx. Their son, John Jr., was born on September 20, 1968. In addition, his sisters Roseann and Dolores, each of whom were considerably younger than Skagen, lived with him after his marriage in 1964. He took them in while they were still children and raised and supported them.

When Skagen became a police officer in 1970, he was a mature man with over a decade of military experience and discipline behind him. He had a wife and a family to care for, and was considered an excellent prospect by the police department.

His work record had borne out this promise. He had gone through his training easily, getting good grades and high evaluations from his instructors. In his work with guns he had received a sharpshooter rating, and was proficient in the use of side arms. Once on active duty, his performance had also been good. His record showed only one disciplinary violation, an altercation between him and a a former boyfriend of one of his sisters. Though no one had been hurt and it was a minor matter, it had been reported to the police, investigated and noted on Skagen's file.

All in all, John Skagen was a good man who was well liked by all who knew him, a decent man who shouldered considerable responsibility without complaint. He was not the sort to become involved casually or frivolously in a dangerous incident.

9

Ballistics

Ballistics evidence accumulated rapidly. Skagen's off-duty revolver was brought downtown as were the service revolvers of Patrolmen Wieber, Jacobsen and Pade. The four bullets, marked *S/U1* to *S/U4*, arrived from the morgue, and the bullet removed from Richardson's back was brought from Lincoln Hospital. Police experts were ready to try to piece together the evidence.

The first step was a test of the four revolvers to determine whether they had been fired recently, and if so, how many times. When a gun is fired, an explosive charge in the rear of the cartridge is set off, propelling the bullet at high speed through the barrel of the gun. This small explosion leaves a telltale residue of powder both in the barrel of the gun and in the chamber housing the cartridge. By determining how many chambers have this residue (a police .38 caliber service revolver has six chambers) an expert will know how many times it has been fired.

Detective Robert Clancy of the Ballistics Section of the

New York City Police Department is such an expert. On the morning of June 29 he examined the four revolvers, and found that Patrolman Wieber had fired all six chambers of his gun, that Patrolman Jacobsen had fired three times, that Patrolman Pade had fired four times and that Patrolman Skagen had fired once.

Next, the five bullets were measured and weighed in an attempt to calibrate them. The caliber of a bullet is a measurement of its diameter. Thus, a .22 caliber bullet is 22 one hundredths of an inch in diameter, a .25 caliber bullet 25 one hundredths and so on. Strangely, a .38 caliber bullet (for reasons best known to the Colt Company) is only 357 one thousandths of an inch in diameter. Still, it is universally known as a .38.

To be successfully fired, the caliber of a bullet must match the caliber of the gun that fires it. A .38 caliber bullet cannot be fired from a .22 caliber pistol, and a .22 caliber bullet cannot be fired from a policeman's service revolver.

The weight of a bullet is more or less standardized by caliber, and as the caliber increases, so does the bullet's weight. When a bullet has struck something, it is often so deformed that its diameter cannot be measured. Then its weight in grams may permit an expert to determine its caliber.

The five bullets were not especially deformed, and the measurements were easy. The bullet removed from Richardson's shoulder turned out to be a .38 caliber bullet, as were the three bullets (S/U2 to S/U4) removed from Skagen's abdomen. The bullet removed from Skagen's shoulder (S/U1) was a .32 caliber slug.

The final test performed was a microscopic comparison of the .38 caliber bullets and the police revolvers. This would determine whether the four bullets had been fired from the same gun and whether they had been fired from any of the four revolvers that had been sent downtown. Such comparisons can be made because the rifling inside the barrel of every revolver is unique. This rifling consists of a pattern of spiral grooves and elevations (called lands) that are gouged into the interior surface of the barrel.

The purpose of this rifling is to impart a gyrating spin to a bullet as it is propelled at high speeds through the barrel. As a bullet moves forward it expands into the grooves and is forced into a spin which has the aerodynamic effect of stabilizing it in its flight much like the spiral of a well-thrown football. Without this spin a bullet would tumble end over end through the air with no accuracy at all.

The pattern of lands and grooves in a gun is standardized by manufacturer and caliber. For instance, a .32 caliber Clerke revolver will always have "left-six" rifling—meaning that it has a pattern of six lands and six grooves arranged so that it will impart a "left twist" or a leftward spin on the bullet. But what makes each individual gun unique is not the rifling but the pattern of the scratches left in the lands and grooves by the tap, or die, that gouges out the grooves in the barrel. These scratches are inevitable, random and unique for each gun. Though insignificant in affecting the flight of a bullet, these scratches are crucial to the microscopic identification of the source of a fired bullet, for they will be indelibly imprinted on its surface. This imprint is a signature which can only be written by one particular gun, and all bullets fired from that gun will have the same signature. Thus, a simultaneous microscopic comparison of these scratches or striations on two bullets under a binocular microscope will permit an expert to determine whether they were fired from the same gun. By test-firing a gun and comparing the test bullet with another, it can be determined whether the second bullet was fired from the tested gun.

A microscopic comparison determined that the three bullets *(S/U2* to *S/U4)* taken from Skagen's abdomen were all fired from Patroman Wieber's gun, and that the bullet removed from Richardson's back was fired by John Skagen. The ballistics experts could make no determination about the origin of Richardson's groin wound or of Skagen's second shoulder wound. In both cases no bullet had been recovered.

10

A True Bill

The grand jury sits in a stately oak-paneled room on the eighth floor of the Bronx County Courthouse. Seated in ornate overstuffed leather chairs, and surrounded by large brass ashtrays and cuspidors, the grand jurors themselves seem to reflect the values of days long past. Twenty-three in number, and mostly middle-aged or older, they sit impassively, asking few questions of the witnesses that parade before them. They are soon numbed by the seemingly endless repetition of violent and depraved tales that they are asked to consider. By the end of a working day they resemble a tired matinée audience rather than a deliberative body.

The grand jury room itself is an amphitheater. There are two elevated semicircular tiers of seats for the grand jurors, while in the well of the room witnesses, assistant district attorneys, stenographers and interpreters perform their various functions. The drama, such as it is, that is enacted in this setting is not exciting, and ordinarily the denouement is predictable—a "true bill" is voted, signifying that the grand jury has, by indictment, formally accused an individual of committing one or more enumerated crimes.

So it was with James Richardson. By July 12, roughly twenty witnesses had been hastily assembled and brought before the grand jury. Interviewed by Assistant District Attorney William Quinn, each individual was shepherded briefly into the amphitheater to testify. Since defense attorneys are never permitted to appear before the grand jury, they were not cross-examined and their respective stories were not challenged. They gave only the bare outlines and then left.

The cast of characters would eventually become a familiar one. Calvin Klinger, Sylvester Farish, Robert Jiminez and Mrs. Betancourt all appeared, as did Patrolmen Pade, Rath, Santiago, Villarubia and Jacobsen. Detectives Gest, Cruz and Arana testified, and then Raul Bianchi, and a group of the adolescents who figured in the gun recovery took their turns on the witness stand. Dr. Herzog, from Lincoln Hospital, and Dr. Uku, from the medical examiner's office, both testified as experts, and so did the men from the ballistics squad. They all marched in and out in rapid succession, each one blurred and then forgotten within minutes.

George Wieber also testified. He arrived with a PBA attorney, and after consultation signed a waiver of immunity. The possibility existed that Wieber himself could be indicted and charged with a criminal offense for his actions at the Hunts Point station. Thus, before he could be permitted to testify, he had to waive the immunity from prosecution which all witnesses before grand juries automatically receive by law. Theoretically, of course, his agreement to testify on a waiver of immunity was purely voluntary, but as a practical matter, he was, like all policemen, hardly in a position to refuse. Though such a refusal would clearly have been his constitutional right, it would just as clearly have cost him his job—a dilemma that then faced all peace officers who are the possible targets of grand jury action. However, Wieber displayed no reluctance, waived immunity and testified.

Richardson did not testify, although he might have done so had he, too, chosen to waive immunity. As a tactical matter, civilian defendants rarely elect to exercise this privilege. Most defense attorneys can see no useful purpose in exposing their clients to extensive one-sided cross-examination by the prosecutor in a closed grand jury session. It is not difficult to imagine that Richardson was advised not to testify.

It took the grand jury less than five minutes to deliberate and return a true bill against James Richardson. The following day an indictment was prepared and in due course it was signed by the foreman of the grand jury and filed with the court. It read as follows:

SUPREME COURT
IN AND FOR THE COUNTY OF BRONX

THE PEOPLE OF THE STATE OF NEW YORK
        against
   JAMES RICHARDSON
        Defendant

THE GRAND JURY OF THE COUNTY OF BRONX, by this indictment accuse defendant, of the CRIME of MURDER committed as follows:

The said defendant, in the County of Bronx, on or about June 28, 1972, while engaged in the commission of a felony, to wit, ESCAPE IN THE SECOND DEGREE, and in the course of such crime, and in furtherance thereof, and in immediate flight therefrom, caused the death of one JOHN SKAGEN, a police officer of the New York City Transit Authority Police department.

SECOND COUNT:

AND THE GRAND JURY AFORESAID, by this indictment, further accuse said defendant of the CRIME of MANSLAUGHTER IN THE SECOND DEGREE committed as follows:

The said defendant, in the County of Bronx, on or about June 28, 1972, recklessly caused the death of the said JOHN SKAGEN, a police officer of the New York City Transit Authority Police Department.

THIRD COUNT:

AND THE GRAND JURY AFORESAID, by this indictment, further accuse said defendant of the CRIME of an ATTEMPT TO COMMIT THE CRIME OF MURDER committed as follows:

The said defendant, in the County of Bronx, on or about June 28, 1972, attempted to cause the death of the said JOHN SKAGEN, a police officer of the New York City Transit Authority Police Department by means of a deadly weapon, to wit, a loaded pistol and revolver.

FOURTH COUNT:

AND THE GRAND JURY AFORESAID, by this indictment, further accuse said defendant of the CRIME of ESCAPE IN THE SECOND DEGREE committed as follows:

The said defendant, in the County of Bronx, on or about June 28, 1972, having been arrested for a felony, escaped from custody.

FIFTH COUNT:

AND THE GRAND JURY AFORESAID, by this indictment, further accuse said defendant of the CRIME of POSSESSING A WEAPON AS A FELONY committed as follows:

The said defendant, in the County of Bronx, on or about June 28, 1972, had in his possession a firearm, to wit, a pistol loaded with ammunition, said possession not being in defendant's home or place of business.

SIXTH COUNT:

AND THE GRAND JURY AFORESAID, by this indictment, further accuse said defendant of the CRIME of RECKLESS ENDANGERMENT IN THE SECOND DEGREE committed as follows:

The said defendant, in the County of Bronx, on or about June 28, 1972, recklessly engaged in conduct which created a substantial risk of serious physical injury to one JOHN JACOBSEN, an officer of the Police Department of the City of New York.

SEVENTH COUNT:

AND THE GRAND JURY AFORESAID, by this indictment, further accuse said defendant of the CRIME of CRIMINAL POSSESSION OF STOLEN PROPERTY IN THE THIRD DEGREE committed as follows:

The said defendant, in the County of Bronx, on or about June 28, 1972, knowingly possessed stolen property, to wit, a New York State Department of Corrections badge, with intent to benefit himself and a person other than the owner thereof, and to impede the recovery of the owner thereof, one MAY ELAINE WILLIAMS.

Burton B. Roberts
District Attorney

Normally an indictment is of little more than symbolic significance. The facts alleged against a defendant are generally clear-cut, and can be easily broken down into specific enumerated crimes. The indictment lists these crimes, and a trial is held to determine whether or not the commission of these alleged crimes can be proved beyond a reasonable doubt.

The Richardson case was that one case in a million which differs from this rule. Everyone involved in the investigation of the Hunts Point subway shooting more or less agreed that James Richardson had committed any number of serious crimes, even if, at this early stage, there was some confusion over precisely what he had in fact done. But from a legal perspective, the known facts of the shoot-out were so bizarre that on the question of what crimes he had committed, the disagreement was complete. Nothing quite like this incident had ever occurred before, and there was no neat precedent or statute to guide the district attorney's office in the drafting of the indictment.

This lack of clear precedents was of more than academic

interest, for the indictment, once filed, would lock the prosecution into a fixed and irrevocable theory of the case. Later, when the case would be moved to trial, the prosecution would be constrained to prove the seven charges of the indictment, no more and no less. Therefore the indictment would, in a sense, define the legal issues of the case.

The time pressures on the prosecution to obtain this indictment were intense. James Richardson was in custody from the moment of his arrest, and without an indictment the law would mandate his release. The prospect of a cop killer being released from custody because of a delay in obtaining an indictment hardly commended itself to Burton B. Roberts, and so, perhaps with greater haste than prudent legal scholars might have desired, an indictment was obtained. Years later, a price would be paid for this haste.

The grand jury did not choose to indict George Wieber. Eventually, the defense would have something to say about this decision.

11

Bail

The Bronx Criminal Courthouse on 161st Street and Washington Avenue is a grim fortress of a building which sits squat and forbidding in the middle of a South Bronx slum. Outside the courthouse, the streets are littered with garbage, broken glass and empty beer cans. Inside, the often-painted walls have long since peeled and faded to a nondescript green. Sporadic cleaning efforts have never succeeded in eliminating either the graffiti or the stale, musty odor of defeat.

The courtrooms themselves are shabby, overcrowded and noisy. Business is conducted there in an atmosphere more reminiscent of a fishmarket than of a court of law. There is none of the wood paneling or muted elegance that one expects of such a place. All the trappings are missing, and so is that indefinable aura which in other courts instills respect for the power and majesty of the law. The atmosphere of the Bronx Criminal Court is the living antithesis of such qualities.

In fairness to the courthouse, it is open seven days a week, almost around the clock, struggling to dispense justice to a caseload so huge and so varied that it defies the imagination. Roughly fifty thousand cases a year, ranging in gravity from murder to loitering, wend their way through the Criminal Court. Of these, perhaps thirty-five hundred are removed by indictment to be prosecuted in the State Supreme Court as felonies; the remainder, from start to finish, are disposed of by the Criminal Court.

Understandably, the single greatest pressure upon the roughly twenty judges who preside over the various parts of the Criminal Court is a permanent and absolute requirement that cases be rapidly disposed of. It takes no great insight to appreciate the fact that if the bulging court calendars are not quickly cleared of existing cases, a backlog would soon develop of such magnitude that the entire criminal justice system would collapse of its own weight.

Presiding over as many as sixty different cases in an eight-hour working day, and ever aware of the pressure to get dispositions, a Criminal Court judge, even if possessed of the wisdom of Solomon, is hard pressed to render true justice. It is difficult enough to sit in judgment when there is time for careful study and reflection. It is hardly the fault of the judiciary that under existing conditions the residents of the Bronx receive a form of bargain-basement justice.

The case of *The People of the State of New York* v. *James Richardson* did not reach the Bronx Criminal Court until July 11. Had Richardson not been injured and hospitalized, he would have been arraigned within twenty-four hours of his arrest. Indeed, while he was still a patient at Lincoln Hospital, arrangements had been made for a judge to travel there for a bedside arraignment, but these plans were called off when the following note was received by the Clerk of the Court:

July 8, 1972

I am an attorney for James Richardson and I cannot be present for an arraignment on Monday July 10, 1972. Because of the seriousness of the anticipated charges against Mr. Richardson, I request that any booking or arraignment proceedings be put off until I am present.

/s/ *William M. Kunstler*
Center for Constitutional
Rights

Kunstler's wishes were honored. After consultation with all concerned, the arraignment was scheduled for July 11.

The formal purpose of an arraignment is to serve notice to a defendant, before a magistrate, of the charges lodged against him. It is also an opportunity for the magistrate to formally advise a defendant of his rights and privileges in defending himself in the case against him. However, these purposes, once most important, are now largely meaningless. There is no time to read each defendant a lengthy litany of charges and rights. Instead, the court relies upon defense lawyers to privately educate their clients to these legal mysteries. In practice, a formal reading of an arraignment is invariably waived.

One crucial issue is confronted at arraignment, an issue that stays with a case from the very outset until the moment of disposition: the question of bail. In a sense, no question can be more important, for at stake is the difference between freedom and incarceration. For a defendant, bail is the bottom line of a criminal case. No power on earth can ever restore to an individual even a single day (or hour, or minute) spent behind bars. In setting bail, a judge, without determining guilt or innocence, is in effect deciding whether or not an individual will be free to continue his everyday life. It is an awesome responsibility.

The way our courts currently deal with the question of bail is generally conceded to be unsatisfactory. Judges are given the impossible task of trying to assign to each case a dollar amount that is sufficiently high to discourage the defendant's flight, while sufficiently low to be both realistically within the defendant's means and also within the constitutional prohibition against excessive bail. Under the existing time pressures, this determination cannot be made intelligently. The result is a haphazard system, based more on whim and happenstance than upon information and logic. Moreover, our bail system discriminates against the poor. A wealthy man, faced even with a serious crime, can post bail, however high, and retain his pre-trial freedom. A poor man, facing even relatively minor charges, may languish in jail for months awaiting trial because he lacks a few hundred dollars.

The consequences of pre-trial detention are particularly grim. The anxiety and uncertainty that preys on the mind of any incarcerated man are acute enough. Add to this the ever-present prospect of either acquittal and freedom, or conviction and a lengthy sentence, and you have created an emotional hell for the accused. There is the anguish of separation from one's family and the special torment of being unable to assist in the preparation of a defense. An accused person desperately needs to go out into his community and help his attorney (usually a mistrusted outsider in that community) to find the witnesses who will bolster the defense. This cannot be done from a jail cell. Statistics have long shown that a jailed defendant is far more likely to be convicted and sent to prison than a defendant who makes bail.

In addition, the conditions in prisons for pre-trial detainees are generally far worse than those for convicted and sentenced prisoners. Opportunities for education and rehabilitation, such as they are, are far fewer for the more transitory population of pre-trial prisoners. Sentenced prisoners at least are aware of the terms that they face, and can begin to adjust emotionally to the realities of their situation. For those awaiting trial, anxiety and uncertainty become contagious, and adjustment or resignation become impossible. The crowning irony, of course, is that these men are presumed to be innocent.

Statute and case law set forth seven criteria which a judge must consider in setting bail: (1) a defendant's character and reputation; (2) his employment and financial resources; (3) his family ties and length of residence in the community; (4) his prior criminal record, if any; (5) his previous record, if any, of responding to court appearance dates in criminal cases; (6) the weight of the evidence against him and the probability of conviction; and (7) the possible sentence faced in the event of a conviction. These criteria did not give Kunstler a great deal to work with.

Richardson had a prior conviction, albeit on a marijuana charge. Actually, there were two warrants out for his arrest: one from his parole violation in Rochester, New York, and one for jumping bail in the Brooklyn Criminal Court. He was, in fact, a double fugitive from justice who had a record of not appearing in court on his cases.

The charges against Richardson were the most serious criminal charges envisioned in the Penal Law. The murder of a police officer was then a capital case, and if convicted on all charges Richardson faced the electric chair. Burton B. Roberts and his staff were quite prepared to argue—and did—that their case was strong, and the likelihood of conviction great. Therefore the prosecution demanded an astronomical bail far in excess of any amount that Richardson could conceivably raise.

Faced with the People's demand, Kunstler was not at a loss for words. Working with what he had, he stressed in moving terms Richardson's work record as a clerk at Lincoln Hospital, belittled his past criminal record as trivial, sneering at the marijuana conviction, and pointed out that his client helped to support five children.

Then, his anger growing, Kunstler moved on to his own version of the case. He asserted (based on what evidence no one knew) that Patrolman Skagen "was shot to death by two New York City policemen," and that Richardson himself had been shot twice by these same arresting officers. For Kunstler, Richardson was an innocent black bystander caught in the toils of the white man's violence. He never let anyone forget that Skagen, Wieber, Jacobsen, Pade and Rath were all white and never mentioned Santiago and Villarubia, both Puerto Rican. As far as Kunstler was concerned, Richardson never possessed a gun and fired no shots. His portrayal of Richardson was masterly.

Faced with these conflicting claims and bald assertions, Criminal Court Judge Louis A. Cioffi set Richardson's bail at $50,000. A week later, on July 18, before another judge, these arguments were repeated and the bail was reduced by $10,000 to $40,000.

By August 2 Richardson had been indicted, and the case had moved to the State Supreme Court. Here, once more, bail arguments were heard, and once again Kunstler summoned forth his anger and eloquence. His words had impact, for bail was reduced once again, this time to $25,000.

There matters stood for some five months. Then, in January of 1973, Kunstler tried again. He succeeded in chopping off another $10,000. Bail was set at $15,000. It never went lower.

These successive drops in bail were arbitrary, but not unusual. Actually, $15,000 bail is an astronomical figure in the South Bronx, a fact that was well known to these judges. Their cuts were in reality little more than a gesture made in response to Kunstler's impassioned arguments. By all existing standards the bail was, and remained, prohibitively high.

12

"This Could Happen to You"

There were a number of people who were ready to come to James Richardson's defense. The news media had given the bizarre events at the Hunts Point station a fair amount of coverage, and word of mouth had done the rest. It was not long before a James Richardson Defense Committee had been formed, and in the South Bronx the case became a minor cause célèbre.

The heart of Richardson's support came, naturally, from his co-workers at Lincoln Hospital. The hospital itself is hardly a stranger to splinter political and social movements of all complexions. Exposed as they are to a constant barrage of the worst outrages and tragedies of ghetto life, many workers at Lincoln Hospital are radicalized, and channel their understandable frustrations and angers into a succession of causes and movements. For them the case was a natural. Even though Richardson himself was not really politically active, he was, after all, one of their own. Besides, from a radical perspective, the political significance of the Richardson case was not difficult to perceive

The first move was to obtain a lawyer. Here, the choice was obvious. There was one name that stood out: William M. Kunstler was the one attorney, the defense committee knew, who could both obtain justice for James Richardson and simultaneously advance and publicize their ideology and cause. Indeed, his notoriety alone was enough to guarantee ample publicity for their side.

Still, it is one thing to want William Kunstler to defend a criminal action for you, and quite another thing to get him. A busy man with a brutal personal caseload (to say nothing of extensive speaking and writing obligations), Kunstler is in far greater demand than he could possibly hope to satisfy. Earning a substantial income from his speaking and writing efforts, he is not dependent upon the practice of law to support himself; consequently, he is most selective in accepting cases.

Nevertheless, Kunstler agreed to take the case. Later, he would state that the case's fact pattern had intrigued him. The idea, as he put it, "of one cop killing another cop, and then charging a black bystander with the crime" appealed to him. It seemed to him a perfect vehicle for just the sort of politicized trial that he relished. As in all such cases, Kunstler agreed to work free of charge.

With an attorney secured, the second step facing the committee was obvious but difficult: money had to be secured for Richardson's bail. Raising ten or twenty thousand dollars is no mean feat in a community where wages are low, prices are high and every fourth person is out of work. But it was done, with the aid of leaflets, such as the following, that were distributed along with a newsletter of the Black Panther Party:

"THIS COULD HAPPEN TO YOU"

On June 28, 1972, James Richardson was on the way to work at Lincoln Hospital where he worked for the last two years as a senior admitting clerk. He rode the Hunts Point route to work the same way he did every working day.

In the Hunts Point Station James saw a white man shooting up the subway. While James was trying to get out of the way of the shooting he was shot twice. He managed to get to the top of the staircase of the subway where he saw two white cops.

James allegedly told the cops that a crazy man was shooting up the subway.

The two cops proceeded to investigate the incident and six shots were fired. The crazy man lay dead with six bullets in him.

Police further investigated the situation and found out that the crazy white man was an off-duty cop, who had just finished performing as an off-duty cop. Immediately, the cops concocted a classic, fascist frame up to hide another morbid act of amerikkkan fascism. So as to confuse the facts, the cops said that Richardson had a gun and patrolman Shagen was acting in the line of duty. The patrolman Shagen tried to arrest Richardson for possession of a gun. The cops had to fabricate the facts in order to put "law and order" in a human context. So by creating a gun that nobody but the cops saw, the cops created a theoretical basis to put James Richardson in the electric chair. The cops and Bronx D.A. Burton Roberts are going to try to prove that if James Richardson created a situation that led to a cop getting killed by other cops, then Richardson is a murderer and the State of New York should execute that murderer, regardless of the fact that it was a crazy man in the Pelham Bay subway that day.

Fascist cops in New York City are some of the most trigger-happy pigs in the world. New York City cops have a consistent history of going beserk and shooting first and asking questions later. Only after the hideous murder of 10-year old Ricky Bodden by New York patrolman Francis Ortolano on August 15, 1972 did the N.Y.P.D. give cops a new regulation about when to shoot their guns. The communities would like to know how that new regulation is going to be enforced, or who's going to police the police, because the murderer of Ricky Bodden is still at large.

In March of this year in Jamaica, Queens, a white cop saw two Black men involved in an incident on N.Y. Boulevard. The white cop shot at the two Black men—killing one of them. After further investigation the facts revealed that the dead man was named William Capers who was a 15-year veteran detective of the New York City police department.

The Queens Grand Jury and Queens D.A. Mackerell said that the white cop who killed Detective Capers did not commit any crime.

In May of this year hoards of fascist pigs of the N.Y.P.D. viciously attacked Muhammad's Mosque #7. The fascists gave the pretext that the N.Y.P.D. received a phone call that said some cops needed assistance on the second floor of the Mosque—which is the Muslim school. The Muslims, under the able leadership of Minister Farrakhan, righteously defended their Mosque from a vicious attack from the N.Y.P.D. death squad. When the smoke cleared at the Mosque, one white cop lay dead from the guns of his fellow cops.

Weeks later Manhattan D.A. Hogan indicted three Muslims for assaulting the dead cop. The reason why the three Muslims were not indicted for murder is because the Nation of Islam is very powerful and respected in the Black community.

James Richardson is not a member of any national or local progressive organization. That's why Bronx District Attorney Roberts thinks it will be easy to railroad James Richardson into the electric chair. The purpose of the James Richardson Defense Committee is to derail the train and stop the railroad by placing James back into the Black community.

We must not forget the incident in Detroit this year when cops from STRESS squad busted into the apartment where six Black men were playing cards. STRESS squad came in the door shooting first and asking questions later. Two Black Wayne County deputies were killed on the spot. Wayne County Grand Jury said that the cops acted in the line of duty. Fortunately the pigs could not think up a James Richardson conspiracy.

The case of James Richardson will illustrate many political, labor and legal contradictions. To the so-called Marxist-Leninists who say that policemen are part of the real proletarian and are oppressed too, we say that James Richardson is a true worker for the people because he worked for the people at Lincoln Hospital, and not against the people (like the pigs do). The Municil/2al Labor Union in which James Richardson is a member denied him his constitutional rights by suspending James from the union immediately after he got arrested. The U.S. Constitution says a person is innocent until proven guilty. When the Municipal Union suspended James before he exhausted due process of law—in who's interest was the union acting for—James Richardson or Bronx D.A. Burton Roberts?

To the people who supported the Harlem 6, Huey Newton, Angela Davis, Carlos Feliciano and the N.Y. 21, we ask you not to hold back your support for James Richardson because he's not a superstar. Justice is more important than limelighting and personalities.

To Burton Roberts and the forces of fascism—we say your legal theory to put James Richardson in the electric chair will be destroyed, just as your theories to put Angela Davis, Huey Newton and the Harlem 6 in the electric chair and gas chamber have failed.

For further information: James Richardson Defense Committee
c/o National Committee for the
Defense of Political Prisoners
P.O. Box 1184
Harlem, N.Y. 10027

Telephone: 993–4500 Ext. 273

By February 1973 enough money had been raised to post bond for Richardson. On February 13, 1973, he was released from custody after spending almost seven months in jail.

13

Justice Delayed

The average jury trial takes roughly two weeks to progress from jury selection to verdict. A homicide trial takes somewhat longer, perhaps three weeks from start to finish. In 1972 alone there were over four hundred homicides committed in Bronx County.

There are only five trial parts of the Supreme Court, Bronx County, that preside over homicide trials. If each of these trial parts were to operate at peak efficiency, five days a week and fifty-two weeks a year (which in fact they do not), it would still be impossible to try more than seventy-five homicide cases each year.

The statistics are bleak. Although the homicide rate is running at more than one a day, the pace of criminal-trial procedures is deliberate, even leisurely. The simple fact of the matter is that in our urban centers—for there is nothing unique about these Bronx statistics—we are utterly unprepared and unequipped to deal justly with street crime. There is a flood of crime and a trickle of trials; in between, in the bowels of the criminal justice system, the pressure builds.

The Constitution of the United States specifically guarantees to every individual accused of a crime the right to a speedy trial. Today that guarantee is a farce. Justice demands that the oldest cases be tried first, and the backlog of untried cases is immense. Since the courts' trial capacities are limited, the average wait, from arrest to trial, for a homicide case in Bronx County is roughly eighteen months. One and a half years is spent before anyone even gets around to determining guilt or innocence, and for most homicide defendants this time is spent in jail.

Who can calculate the injustice worked upon defendants by this delay? Apart from the anxiety and torment of pre-trial incarceration in general, the fact remains that a significant number of these defendants who do go to trial are ultimately vindicated by an acquittal. What does one say to a man who has spent eighteen months in jail waiting for an acquittal— "I'm sorry"? This is just not good enough, but it is precisely what happens again and again.

Over the years the courts have been peppered with "speedy trial" motions brought by homicide defendants who are seeking to dismiss the cases against them for "failure to prosecute." These motions are routinely answered by the district attorney's office by pointing to the huge caseload and the small trial capacity of the courts, and by promising to try all cases in chronological order. Such dismissal motions are just as routinely denied by the courts, none of which are prepared to face the public outcry that would surely result if accused murderers were released en masse. It doesn't take much imagination to visualize newspaper headlines characterizing such a decision as a "legalized jailbreak." Such realities ensure that delay will continue.

Ironically, delay is a double-edged sword that as often hurts the prosecution and helps the defendant as the other way around. Prosecutors hate delay, for it inevitably weakens and sometimes even destroys their cases. In time, memories fade, or disappear altogether. Often important witnesses vanish, lose interest or die. The passage of time has ruined many strong cases, and many a guilty man has been acquitted because of delay.

In the final analysis, delay is an unmitigated flaw of the criminal justice system. It hurts the innocent, and gives comfort to the guilty. It serves no useful purpose.

It took over twenty-seven months for the Richardson case to be moved to trial. This delay, almost a full year longer than the intolerable average of eighteen months, was in no way the responsibility or fault of either the courts or the district attorney's office. In fact no one could truly be said to be at fault for the delay. It was occasioned for the most part by the tremendous caseload and inevitable scheduling difficulties of William Kunstler.

From the first, Kunstler proved to be an elusive figure. Rarely, if ever, did he appear in person at the numerous calendar calls for the case; instead, James Richardson would show up, clutching in his hand an affidavit signed by Kunstler, explaining that he was committed elsewhere and would be for some time. Invariably he would ask for lengthy adjournments because of his other engagements.

Richardson was free on bail after February 13, 1973. Thereafter, the victim of this enormous delay was the district attorney's office. It was this office that would bear the burden of proof at the eventual trial, and it was the district attorney whose witnesses' credibility became increasingly subject to attack with each passing month. Kunstler, the man who would be doing the attacking, was far too experienced a defense lawyer not to be aware of the tactical advantages of delay. In time it became clear that he was in no hurry to move the Richardson case to trial.

Then came Wounded Knee. In 1973 a group of American

Indians illegally seized some property at Wounded Knee, South Dakota, primarily to publicize the accumulated injustices that they felt they had suffered at the hands of American society in general and the federal government in particular. Police forces had responded to the seizure, a siege resulted, and some people were injured.

The inevitable federal prosecutions followed, and perhaps just as inevitably William Kunstler became the chief defense attorney for those accused. The trial that followed became an extravaganza that dragged on for nine long months. At the beginning of the Wounded Knee trial Kunstler had promised to follow it immediately with the Richardson case. But contrary to his representations that it would not be a lengthy trial, Wounded Knee dragged on month after month, leaving both the Bronx court and the district attorney powerless. Finally, in September of 1974, Wounded Knee came to a bizarre conclusion when a juror fell ill and the jury was unable to reach a verdict. Within a week the Richardson case was moved to trial before the Honorable Ivan Warner in Part 21 of the Bronx Supreme Court.

14

The Education of an Assistant District Attorney

Nothing in my background even vaguely prepared me for the shocks that I experienced upon becoming an assistant district attorney. Essentially sheltered, the product of suburban public schools, Williams College and Columbia Law School, my upbringing was far removed from the harsh realities of urban law enforcement. No course of study had prepared me to stand in a South Bronx alleyway at 4 A.M. on a summer morning and look at the mutilated body of a fifteen-year-old gang member. Pleasant summers in the Catskills and the Berkshires did not equip me to take a confession from a woman who had just drowned her year-old infant in boiling water. My law school professors had not taught me what to say to an eighty-three-year-old woman whose husband of sixty-one years had just been stabbed to death by two fourteen-year-old girls. My middle-class complacency was of no help in allaying the fears of an old man, twice mugged, who was now afraid to go out to the corner for groceries. In short, I was woefully unprepared to become an assistant district attorney.

My motives for becoming an assistant district attorney in the first place were mixed. I might have followed the majority of my law school class into a comfortable and lucrative corporate practice in Manhattan. At the time, however, I wanted something more interesting—something active, something that would get me into the "real world." The district attorney's office seemed to be the answer to these needs. Moreover, I had known throughout law school that I wanted to be a trial lawyer. I fancied the idea of courtroom drama, and in my mind's eye I had no difficulty envisioning myself doing great things. I was ambitious and impatient.

Burton B. Roberts, then the District Attorney of Bronx County, impressed me. He was flamboyant and charismatic, and enjoyed a reputation for building a young, nonpolitical and highly professional prosecutor's office in Bronx County. I liked him when I met him, and when he offered me the chance to advance rapidly and assume great responsibility as a public servant, I accepted, and became an assistant district attorney.

The truth of the matter is that I did not give a great deal of thought to my decision to become a prosecutor. I had some vague ideas, but in reality I just drifted into the job. Roberts made me an offer, there was nothing available at the time that seemed better, and I accepted it; it was as simple as that. I didn't have the faintest idea of what I was getting into.

My first exposure to the office was tame enough. I was assigned to the Appeals Bureau to do legal research and to write briefs. The first trials I ever saw were on paper, transcripts of cases that had been tried and won by other assistant district attorneys. My job was to defend these convictions and to try to prevent reversals in the appellate courts. The Appeals Bureau was the easiest place to make the transition from the academic to the real world.

However, even in the gentle, rarefied atmosphere of the Appeals Bureau I was quickly exposed to the harsh realities of criminal law. I was taught that the rigorous, intellectually pure law that I had been taught at law school had to be discarded —or at least modified—to conform to the imperfect and all-too-human standards around me. I soon learned that to be an effective appellate advocate you had to appeal as much to a judge's gut as to his intellect. I came to realize that even in the most technical appeals, based entirely upon dry and abstract issues of law, emotion could be put to good effect.

For instance, in one appeal based entirely upon the technical propriety of the wording of an indictment, I was instructed to stress to the appellate judges the fact that the defendant in question had been tried and convicted upon overwhelming evidence of selling large quantities of heroin to junior high school students. This fact had nothing to do with the legal issues raised by the defendant seeking a reversal of his conviction, but it could have everything to do with the outcome of the appeal. Appellate courts, I came to learn, are both fallible and human, and it is no secret that a legal issue that will overturn a conviction for a man accused of shoplifting will not necessarily produce the same result for a convicted murderer Theoretically this should not be so; in reality, it inescapably is the case. It is a measure of my naïveté that I was surprised by this realization.

In the summer of 1972, at about the time that John Skagen was killed, I was transferred to the Criminal Court Bureau. I was there for three months and it was a very long and very hot summer for me. The Bronx Criminal Court was a crucible which melted down and transformed my sensibilities. There was no time to even attempt to do justice to the cases that came before me. There was no real information available upon which to make intelligent—let alone fair—decisions. There was nothing except a vast caseload, and a never-ending pressure to dispose of it rapidly. I saw judges with great reputations as civil libertarians threaten defendants in minor cases, and sometimes even withhold realistic bail from them, in an effort to force the guilty pleas that would beef up their so-called "batting average" of dispositions. I saw some defense lawyers put off, or even destroy, dispositions favorable to their clients because they had not "been visited by Mr. Green"—meaning that they had not yet been paid their fees.

Most of all, I saw the victims and I saw the defendants. Every day there were thirty, forty, or fifty new faces, each one unique and yet each one expressing the same hostility, fear and bewilderment at being caught up in the toils of the criminal justice system. In a short time the faces became faceless, and the cases began to merge with one another in my mind. I came to understand what it was to be powerless. The defendants and victims were powerless, and it dawned on me that I, too, was powerless, unable in the final analysis to do anything to appreciably improve the quality of life in Bronx County.

I gained much self-knowledge that summer. Some of it was not pretty. I learned graphically that I had my own weaknesses and fallibilities, and I discovered that, try though I might, I was not always objective and dispassionate in the evaluation of my cases. My likes and my dislikes could affect my judgment, and it was humbling to realize that something as trivial as the state of my digestion might have an influence on whether or not a man went to jail. I came to realize how truly difficult it is to be just.

I also learned, during the summer John Skagen died, to be quick on my feet in a courtroom. Handling forty or more new cases each day proved to be an effective way to sharpen my ability to concentrate. I learned to interview potential witnesses quickly and effectively, and how to question them on the stand. In the rough-and-tumble practice before the Criminal Court, my callowness and inexperience were quickly worn away. If I developed nothing else that summer, I emerged with a certain amount of surface poise and self-assurance

In the fall of 1972 I was promoted to the Supreme Court bureau to try felony cases before juries, and I have been doing so ever since At first I was assigned to the general run of felonies—burglaries, robberies, rapes and assaults. In January 1974 I was again promoted, this time to the Homicide Bureau, and since then I have tried only murder cases.

There was no particular reason why I was assigned to try the Richardson case. In January 1974 Bill Quinn left the district attorney's office and I took over all of his cases in the Homicide Bureau. The Richardson case had been assigned to Quinn. I inherited it.

I remember moving into a new office, throwing my things into an empty metal desk and taping a large paper calendar to the bare yellow walls. It was a tiny office, roughly ten feet long and eight feet wide. In my eighty square feet of space there was barely enough room for a desk, a file cabinet, two chairs and a wastepaper basket. The office was one of six created by the partitioning of a larger room. In an area originally designed for one assistant district attorney, there were now five homicide assistants and one secretary.

The noise and commotion of five active trial lawyers working in such close quarters was deafening. Telephones never stopped ringing, police officers and witnesses were constantly coming and going, the air was always heavy with stale cigarette smoke, and the carpeting was stained with spilled coffee. My office was not a place conducive to serious work. Nevertheless, I was delighted with it, for the office was a vast improvement over my earlier accommodations.

There is an undeniable mystique about working in the Homicide Bureau. It is the senior trial bureau in the office, and is generally conceded to have the most able and experienced assistant district attorneys. Even in the South Bronx, where street crime is so common that it is the norm rather than an aberration, murder is still something special, the ultimate predatory crime. No other crime is as serious or more awful or as feared.

To work the Homicide Bureau is to be constantly exposed

to the very worst that humanity has to offer. Violent and unnatural death is a daily concern. Working Homicide leaves its mark, and one is never quite the same again. Of course, I didn't realize this when I entered the bureau. I saw the trial of a murder case as the greatest challenge there was to the skills of a criminal lawyer. I knew that juries were particularly demanding in murder cases, that they tended to be very cautious and hard to persuade. I knew that murder cases were particularly difficult cases to prosecute, if for no other reason than that there is no victim in a murder case who can come forward and identify the perpetrator of the crime. I was eager to try my first murder case.

On the day I became a Homicide assistant, Millie, the bureau's good-natured secretary, carried thirty-two blue folders into my office. Each folder contained the file of a separate homicide case awaiting trial. The Richardson case was only one of these thirty-two.

I do not remember precisely when I first became aware of the Richardson case. Bill Quinn had spoken to me briefly before he left, and I recall his saying something about Kunstler and a "cop killing" case. However, he said a great deal about many cases, and I had no time to really absorb any of it. There were a number of cases in my files even older, cases in which the defendant was not out on bail. I turned to them first.

Within a month I was in the middle of my first murder trial, a particularly sordid and difficult case involving a nineteen-year-old defendant who was the president of the Imperial Bachelors, a Puerto Rican youth gang. He had shot a member of his own gang, a fifteen-year-old, in the back of the head. The victim had violated the gang's rules; he had been caught using narcotics without the express permission of the president. For this transgression he had been summarily executed.

It was a difficult trial. Most of my witnesses were gang members who were inarticulate and hostile. Each of them was a horrible witness, and to say the least, they did not cut figures in court calculated to instill either respect or belief in the minds of most jurors. I had my hands full just getting these witnesses into court at all. Trying any case is an absorbing experience, and this particular one had me completely preoccupied.

Late one afternoon in the middle of the trial, when court had adjourned for the day, Pat Skagen called. Her voice was soft, polite, even a bit shy, and I could sense that it had not been easy for her to make the call. But what struck me, even then, was a certain quality of quiet determination. Something both gentle and firm in her way of speaking commanded attention. She wanted to know what was happening to her husband's case.

I did not recognize the name Skagen. I did not know what case she was asking about, and at that moment I had neither the time nor the energy to spend talking to her. Calculating that my trial had roughly ten days left to run, I made an appointment to see her in two weeks, wrote a note on my desk calendar, and then forgot all about it.

The jury in that first murder case spent two full days deliberating before they reached a verdict. For over forty-eight hours they were sequestered, and there was nothing to do but hang around the empty courtroom and wait. I made small talk with the defense attorney, read the newspapers and did the crossword puzzles—but for the most part I just waited. It was the most unpleasant part of the trial.

The defendant was waiting too. He was sick as a dog. Pale and in obvious distress, about every fifteen minutes he had to run off to the bathroom to throw up. His family tried to comfort him.

At long last the buzzer rang. Eleven men and one woman filed down into the almost empty courtroom. They all stared away, grim-faced, conscious of the terrible secret they were about to share with us. In silence we all assumed instinctively the roles that our positions demanded.

"Members of the jury, have you reached a verdict?"

The foreman rose. "Yes, your Honor."

"How say you to the first count of the indictment, charging the defendant with the crime of murder—guilty, or not guilty?

"Guilty, your Honor."

The defendant's mother, a little woman dressed in black with a wrinkled face, let out a scream. It was a high, almost unearthly scream, and it seemed to contain all the grief in the world. She was carried from the courtroom by family members and again there was silence.

The jury was polled individually, and one by one each juror stood up and said, "Yes, your Honor, my verdict is guilty." Then the judge thanked them and they filed out as quietly as they had entered. The judge set a date for sentence and then it was all over.

The defendant stood through it all. Silent, staring straight ahead, he didn't seem to hear his mother's scream. It was impossible to say whether he recognized the significance of what had just happened. Oddly enough, he no longer appeared to be ill; perhaps the verdict, even a guilty verdict, was a relief. He was led away by the court officers, now a convicted murderer, no longer presumed to be innocent. He faced a mandatory life sentence.

I realized all this, and it made me sick. Throughout the long weeks of the trial I had been absorbed in courtroom tactics and the daily give-and-take of presenting my case, and I had lost sight of some of the ultimate consequences of the trial. There was no doubt in my mind that the defendant was a vicious killer, and that the people of Bronx County ought to be protected from his future actions. I believed that the jury had reached the correct verdict, and I did not feel that the resulting sentence was unjust. Still, at the moment of that first murder verdict, I became aware of another reality. I saw that the defendant, whatever his crimes, was no less human than I, and I was made to hear, in the mother's scream, the terrible reality of the punishment that would be exacted upon him. In the face of this, all pleasure in my "victory" vanished. I was very troubled as I went home that evening.

The following morning, still shaken by what had happened, I received the congratulations of my colleagues. It had been a "good win," and the news of the verdict had enhanced my reputation. I felt odd about this, but played the game and accepted the compliments. In the middle of this I got a message that Mrs. Skagen was outside to see me. I was pulling out the Richardson file when she entered my office. She was tall, thin and pretty, a young woman in her late twenties or early thirties, with dark hair, sharp features and an expressive face. Her eyes seemed gray and had the same soft yet determined quality as her voice. I liked her immediately.

Understandably, Pat Skagen had an almost obsessive interest in the Richardson case. She wanted to know why the case had not yet gone to trial, why the defendant was not in jail, why Bill Quinn was no longer assigned to the case, and why it had been assigned to me. She wanted to know what I had done to prepare the case. She was polite and soft-spoken, but her eyes gave her away. At length she said, "Look, I'm bringing up my son alone now. He's much too young to understand, but already he's beginning to ask questions. I've got to know the whole truth about what happened to my husband. I want to be able to answer my son's questions. That's why I'm here. I'm going to come to the trial of my husband's murderer."

I tried to answer Mrs. Skagen's questions. In the following months she spent almost as much time in my office as I did, and eventually she got her answers.

15

Preparing a Case

The Richardson case was a trial lawyer's dream. It was also a trial lawyer's nightmare. Complex and emotion-charged, it had dozens of practical problems that had to be overcome, but it also had dozens of strengths to be exploited in court. It was a beautiful case, but one that would require an enormous amount of time and effort.

Unfortunately, time and effort were two items in very short supply in the Homicide Bureau just then. Our backlog was staggeringly large, and was growing. Our shortage of manpower and the pressure on us to dispose of cases quickly was so great that I knew that I could not easily spend a protracted period of time preparing the case. I also knew that nothing less than a lengthy and meticulous preparation would produce results.

I took my problem to Kevin Gilleece, the head of the Homicide Bureau. He could scarcely afford to let me concentrate on a single case, even one concerning a "cop killing," for a couple of months. Still, he promised me the time to prepare and try the case properly. In the months that followed, there was unending pressure on me to turn my attention to other matters, but Kevin kept his promise and assigned new cases to other members of the bureau.

My second problem was easier to solve. I needed a top-notch team of detectives to assist me in preparing the case. Though normally there might be resistance from police officials about removing talented men from active investigations for "mere" trial preparation, such reluctance wouldn't exist for something like the Richardson case. A police officer had been shot to death, and the Police Department would cooperate fully. I acquired the finest team of detectives that I had ever worked with.

Dom Cuccio and Bob Maguire of the Transit Police Detective Division handled much of the administrative and paper work that had to be done. Painstaking and meticulous—traits that are notably lacking in many seasoned detectives—they spent endless hours assembling and cataloging all the documents and physical evidence that would ultimately be used at trial. They had an exact scale model of the Hunts Point subway station built and obtained charts and aerial photographs of the surrounding area. When the time came to present the case to a jury, their efforts paid off handsomely. I was able, with the exhibits they had prepared, to demonstrate graphically how the events at the subway station unfolded that afternoon. The many photographs, charts and models made it easy for the jury to visualize things that might have been very confusing had there been only oral testimony. Cuccio and Maguire had done their jobs superbly.

Hank Arana, Luis Cruz, Juan Caban and Richard Gest handled "the street" (as opposed to "the paper") end of the investigation. Gest, the only homicide detective in the group, brought his special expertise to the case. Arana, Cruz and Caban, the same team that had attempted to track down Richardson's gun, were assigned to the unenviable task of trying to locate the many civilian witnesses after a twenty-month hiatus. In a population as mobile and transient in its living arrangements as the people of the South Bronx, it is no small tribute to the skills of these detectives that by the time of trial every single witness we sought had been located and was available to testify.

My problems were not logistical. I had time and manpower. What I really needed were the answers to a host of questions. I had to know what had actually occurred at the Hunts Point station on the afternoon of June 28, 1972. I knew that John Skagen had been killed, and that James Richardson had been shot twice. But I did not know the exact sequence of events that led to Skagen's death, or what had set them in motion. Events unfolded in split seconds that afternoon. My witnesses had been startled and unprepared for what they had seen. Even minutes after the incident they were uncertain of the details of what they had observed, and since then almost two years had elapsed.

To begin with, I had to find out whether Richardson or Skagen had fired first. This was fundamental, for on the answer would rest my rebuttal to Richardson's certain self-defense claim. But it was a question that no witness could answer for me. All that they had seen were two men with their guns out. They had heard shots, but none of them could say which man had opened fire. In fact, none of them was clear on how many shots had been exchanged all together.

In his various confessions, Richardson had insisted that Skagen had shot him in the groin before he fired back. It was possible that Richardson was correct, but it was so obviously a self-serving statement that it had to be viewed with skepticism. I was certainly not going to rely upon the defendant's word alone.

The truth of the matter eventually emerged from the ballistics and medical evidence. As it turned out, Richardson had fired the first shot. The key evidence proved to be the ballistics examination of Skagen's revolver which revealed that he had fired only once during the entire incident, and that that bullet had been removed from above Richardson's shoulder blade.

Witnesses were quite certain that Skagen had fired a shot up the subway stairs at the fleeing Richardson. The trajectory of such a bullet would have been upward, and in view of Richardson's flight, would have struck him in the side or the back. The path of Richardson's upper wound, striking the rear of the left shoulder and lodging behind the shoulder blade, was consistent with such an upward shot.

Moreover, if Skagen fired his only shot as Richardson ran up the stairs, it followed that Richardson had done all of the firing within the subway station. The evidence seemed to indicate that he had fired four shots in total. Raul Bianchi had found four spent shells and one live round in the .32 caliber revolver he had picked up in the railroad yard near the spot where Richardson had thrown his revolver. The revolver Bianchi found had the brand name Clerke printed on its handle, and .32 caliber Clerkes have left-six rifling. The .32 caliber bullet *(S/U1)* recovered from Skagen's shoulder during the autopsy also had left-six rifling, so it seemed reasonable to conclude that the revolver Bianchi found had belonged to Richardson, and the four spent shells suggested that he had fired four times.

One of these four shots clearly hit Skagen in the shoulder, causing the wound from which the .32 caliber bullet had been recovered. The medical evidence suggested that Skagen's second shoulder wound, the in-and-out wound from which no bullet had been recovered, was also caused by one of Richardson's shots. In addition to being in the same part of Skagen's anatomy, this wound had the same right-to-left path of entry. On the other hand, the three abdominal wounds caused by Patrolman Wieber *(S/U2* to *S/U4)*, traveled from left to right and sharply downward. Had Wieber fired the bullet which caused the in-and-out wound, it would probably have traveled the same right-to-left path as his other three bullets. The inference seemed clear that Richardson had shot Skagen not once but twice.

Richardson said that Skagen had shot him in the groin, but this was impossible, since Skagen had fired only once and had hit Richardson's shoulder. Still, Richardson had insisted that he received his groin wound in the subway station, and this was corroborated by some witnesses who recalled that Richardson ran with a limp from the very beginning, long before Patrolmen Pade and Jacobsen began to fire at him. This was further corroborated by the medical evidence. The path of Richardson's groin wound was at so sharp a downward, almost vertical angle that it could not have been inflicted during the course of the chase. The gun which caused this wound must have been pointed toward the ground at the time it was fired. Had Pade and Jacobsen pointed their guns in such a fashion, they would have shot themselves, rather than a fleeing figure some thirty to fifty yards distant.

This left only one possibility. Richardson had shot himself in the groin while trying to remove the gun from his waistband. It was logical. The gun in his waistband was pointed toward the ground, and a bullet fired from it would have had a trajectory similar to the path of Richardson's groin wound. Ballistics experts confirmed that a .32 caliber Clerke was a hair-triggered gun that discharged easily, and that such guns often caused self-inflicted wounds similar to the injury the defendant had suffered. Given Richardson's undoubted excitement and haste in the subway station that afternoon, it was clear that he had shot himself.

On the basis of this analysis I was able to reconstruct the sequence of events in the subway station. Skagen had forced Richardson against the wall and was about to frisk him when the suspect reached in his waistband and drew his gun, in the process shooting himself in the groin. Richardson fired three more shots, two of which struck Skagen in the shoulder. A chip of cement probably dislodged by the ricocheting final bullet injured Sylvester Farish. Richardson then ran, and Skagen gave chase, firing only once. His shot hit Richardson in the left shoulder as he ran up the stairs. Then Patrolman Wieber shot Skagen three times in the abdomen. That was the whole story.

We had more or less reconstructed the events in the subway station, and the reconstruction was reasonably convincing. However, we were never really able to come up with a completely satisfying answer to the question of why the incident took place at all. To this day I am not certain of why John Skagen decided to stop Richardson in the first place, or why Richardson, with a gun pointed at his back, would elect to draw his own revolver and shoot it out with a police officer. I made some progress with these questions, but in the end all of the pieces never did fall into place.

The first unsolved mystery was Skagen's presence on the token-booth level of the subway station. The Hunts Point subway station has three separate levels: a street level, a token-booth level where passengers go through the turnstiles, and a platform level where they wait for the trains. By all logic, John Skagen had no reason being anywhere other than on the platform level. He had entered the subway system in downtown Manhattan, and his ultimate destination was farther uptown in the Bronx. His only reason for being at the station was to switch from the express to the local, and this switch could be accomplished simply by walking ten steps from one side of the platform to the other.

Why had Skagen walked up the stairs to the token-booth level and to his death? Pat Skagen said that her husband knew no one living in the Hunts Point area, and had no reason she could imagine for leaving the subway there. The station is only a seven-minute ride on the northbound IRT local from the Skagen home, and at 5 P.M., a peak rush hour, this local runs every few minutes. All told, being only minutes away from home and dinner, it seemed unlikely that Skagen would have gone up to the token-booth level to make a telephone call, buy a candy bar or a newspaper, or to use the toilet.

Richardson, on the other hand, lived near the Hunts Point station, and it was natural for him to pass through the token-booth level on his way from the street to the train. He was on his way to work that afternoon, and would have to take the southbound train to reach Lincoln Hospital. This eliminated the possibility of Skagen and Richardson having met on the platform level. The Hunts Point station has two platforms, one northbound and one southbound, and normally the two men would not have met. Still, one way or another, it was certain John Skagen and James Richardson crossed paths that afternoon, and did so on the token-booth level of the station.

The next question, equally difficult to answer, was one of motive. What prompted John Skagen to attempt to place James Richardson under arrest? What was it that Skagen saw? Why did he act?

Richardson's explanation for the confrontation was simple: he felt that Skagen had seen and reacted to the gun tucked in his belt. At least this is what he had told Detective Gest that night at Lincoln Hospital. However, that afternoon Richardson was wearing a dashiki, a long flowing type of shirt worn outside the trousers, that should have effectively concealed the gun he was carrying. Just the same, Richardson's explanation to Detective Gest of Skagen's motivation was the best one that emerged.

It took no clairvoyant to foresee what William Kunstler would claim Skagen's motivation was. I fully expected him to assert that Skagen had approached Richardson because of the racial antagonism that, in Kunstler's view, white police officers —any white police officer—felt toward black civilians. Therefore I explored this possibility thoroughly while preparing my case, but could find no basis whatsoever for the theory that Skagen might have been so motivated. I interviewed the officers who had worked with the dead man—black and Puerto

Rican as well as Irish and Italian—and they all asserted that they had never observed any prejudice in Skagen. More to the point, his police record itself—the arrests he had made and the civilian complaints filed against him (there were remarkably few of these)—was totally devoid of any indication of brutality or racial prejudice. Skagen's friends and acquaintances all confirmed this lack of bias. He had been a normal young man. Not a saint, but there was simply no evidence of bigotry in his background. Kunstler might claim that it existed. I was confident that he could not prove it.

I also explored the possibility that Skagen and Richardson had known each other, and that their meeting that afternoon had had some undisclosed and premeditated purpose. An exhaustive search of the backgrounds of both men failed to reveal any possible relationship between them; as far as could be determined, on the afternoon of June 28, 1972, John Skagen and James Richardson were total strangers.

We speculated that Richardson might have been using his stolen badge to try to "beat" the subway fare. By displaying their badges, policemen are permitted on the subway free of charge. It was not far-fetched to suppose that Richardson, who was carrying a stolen correction officer's badge, might have tried this, and it was equally reasonable to suppose that Skagen, as a Transit Authority patrolman, would be particularly alert to such a subterfuge. It would be the sort of thing that might catch his attention and prompt a confrontation. But though it seemed an excellent explanation for Skagen's action, there was no way of verifying this theory. The only person who could speak with assurance about John Skagen's motives was the man himself.

Richardson's motivation for turning and shooting it out with a policeman was somewhat easier to fathom. There were two warrants out for his arrest on June 28, 1972: one for bail-jumping in a stolen-car case in Brooklyn, the other for a violation of the terms of his probation in Rochester, New York.

If caught, Richardson faced the strong possibility of going to jail for one or both of these cases. In addition, he had an unlicensed revolver concealed on his person. Street-wise, Richardson surely knew that, if discovered, the gun alone might cost him, as an ex-convict and a parole violator, up to seven years in the state penitentiary. In the mind of James Richardson, these were undoubtedly excellent reasons for trying to shoot it out with Skagen and escape.

Almost three years after it occurred I reopened the investigation of the robbery of Marzan's Bar. I knew that the likelihood of solving a crime that was stale and forgotten in the files of the 41st Precinct was remote. Nevertheless, we were all struck by the almost uncanny resemblance between the description of the tall moon-faced robber and James Richardson's appearance. I asked Hank Arana to see whether he could determine if Richardson had participated in the robbery.

In a sense, the connection was somewhat illogical. If James Richardson had indeed robbed Marzan's Bar, he certainly would not have been likely to have called May Elaine Williams to return her identification papers to her. On the other hand, knowing that Richardson had lied to Mrs. Williams and had kept the badge that had been stolen from her, his efforts to reach her made no sense, to begin with. Then again, Richardson's story to Mrs. Williams that he found her papers on the street was not very credible. In fact, the entire incident, telegram and all, was bizarre, and it seemed prudent to try to discover whether Richardson had anything to do with the robbery.

As I anticipated, we came up with nothing. Too much time had passed, the witnesses to the robbery had completely forgotten the appearance of the robbers, and there was no way to determine whether Richardson had been involved.

The preparations for trial took a long time. Questions that were easy to ask proved difficult to answer, and interviewing and preparing my witnesses to testify seemed an endless task. Each of them, civilians and police officers, had to be brought into my office to be interviewed and then reinterviewed. I read to many of them the transcripts of their grand jury testimony, as well as notes of their statements taken by detectives many months before. I asked them to dredge through their memories for any shred of evidence that they might have observed which had been overlooked. It was a painstaking process. Slowly my preparations began to bear fruit. In time I came to feel that I had a command of the evidence that was available to me, and I began to turn my attention to more technical matters.

16

Cause of Death

Death is a concept that is at once simple and complex. It is a word that needs no definition, for we all know what is meant by death. It is also a word that cannot really be defined. Wise men have always argued about the meaning of death, and no doubt always will.

What constitutes the moment of death? Is it when the heart no longer beats? Is it the cessation of breath? Or is it the termination of brain function—the total loss of intelligence, emotion and personality? There are no clear-cut answers to these questions, either medically or legally; they are subject to debate.

Then there is the question of the cause of death. What causes a man's death? The easiest answer is that his heart stopped beating. Why did his heart stop beating? Perhaps the muscles and tissues of the heart failed to receive the blood that it needed to function. Why did it receive insufficient blood? Because the man had been shot five times and bled heavily. Therefore, his death was caused by five bullet wounds.

Such was the logic of the medical examiner's office. Skagen had bled to death. No vital organ had been injured by any of the five bullets, and he might very well have survived any single one of them. Indeed, he very nearly survived all five. It was the opinion of the medical examiner that Skagen's death had been caused by the cumulative effect of all the wounds. The only thing that could be said with certainty was that he died in the way he did. There was no sure way of knowing whether fewer wounds or different wounds would have had the same fatal results. Answers to such questions could only be speculative.

Still, these questions had to be asked, for the trial jury would surely want to know whether it was Richardson or Wieber whose bullets had killed John Skagen. It was important to discover the extent of the damage of the two shoulder injuries directly inflicted by Richardson, and of the three abdominal shots fired by Wieber. To find the answers to these questions, I spent a great deal of time interviewing physicians both in and out of the medical examiner's office.

It turned out that neither the shoulder nor the abdominal wounds were necessarily fatal; in fact, all of the wounds taken together were not necessarily fatal. There were numerous recorded instances of individuals surviving injuries even more extensive, as well as many cases of death resulting from injuries that seemed far less serious than Skagen's. The ability to survive violent trauma, I learned, is a purely individual phenomenon. Some die hard, struggling against massive injury; others go easily, without a fight. No one is quite sure why this is so.

Just the same, there were some things that could be said about Skagen's injuries. Far and away the most serious of them was the tear in the left external iliac artery caused by one of Wieber's .38 caliber bullets *(S/U4)*. This is the major artery that feeds blood from the heart to the legs and lower torso, and it was through this tear that Skagen lost by far the largest amount of blood. It was the single injury that was likely to produce rapid death.

I asked the physicians whether Skagen would have died had he received only the abdominal injuries, and not the shoulder wounds, and was told that there was no sure way of knowing. Most physicians seemed to feel that it was possible and even likely that he would have died, but none of them could be certain.

Then I reversed the question, and asked whether the two shoulder wounds alone could have caused death. The answer was that it was conceivable, but highly unlikely. Of course, it was possible that complications resulting from these wounds—infection, clotting and the like—could have caused death, but Skagen had not lived long enough for these complications to develop.

In the final analysis, all that could be said of the two shoulder wounds was that they had contributed to death. Skagen had come so close to surviving the five wounds that the significance of the two shoulder wounds could not be ignored. Indeed, when Skagen had been wheeled into the operating room the surgeons had properly elected to open up his chest and explore the damage done by the upper wounds before they opened up his abdomen. In so doing, they lost precious minutes before they treated the serious bleeding. In a race as closely run as the surgeons' efforts to save Skagen's life, it was entirely possible that those few lost minutes had made all the difference. Without these shoulder wounds, Skagen might have been saved.

But, of course, this was pure speculation. All that was certain was that the five injuries had each contributed, to a greater or lesser extent, to Skagen's death.

17

The Law of the Case

Getting ready for trial was not simply a question of collecting and assembling evidence. After I had gained a reasonably sure idea of what had actually happened, I had to come to grips with a formidable set of legal problems. In short, I had to find the legal arguments that would persuade the judge who would eventually preside over the Richardson case that the bizarre facts I could prove constituted the seven familiar, well-defined crimes enumerated in the indictment. If I were to fail in my arguments, I would never even get my case to a jury. An unconvinced judge could—and surely would—dismiss the case at the end of the presentation of the People's evidence.

In most cases the legal arguments are relatively cut-and-dried, with standardized patterns and well-established legal precedents. The Richardson case was that one in a million that deviated from this rule. Its pattern was so complex and so bizarre that no legislature and no court that I could find had ever considered anything like it. There simply was no legal precedent available to state either that the provable facts of the

Richardson case consituted the seven crimes of the indictment or that they did not. To a large extent, my researches were taking me into uncharted legal seas. I relished the voyage.

To be sure, the lesser charges of the indictment were not difficult to argue. For instance, there was no real question that there was enough evidence to prove that Richardson had had illegal possession of Mrs. Williams' badge. Certainly the badge had been stolen from Mrs. Williams, and it was equally easy to prove, especially since he had spoken to Mrs. Williams, that Richardson must have been aware that the badge was stolen. It followed that Richardson had no intention of returning the badge to Mrs. Williams. These points, if proved, established the crime of "Criminal Possession of Stolen Property in the Third Degree," the seventh count of the indictment.

Equally simple, from a legal point of view, was the felony gun charge. Many witnesses in the subway station and on the street, civilians and police officers, could testify that they had seen Richardson with a gun. Several had heard it go off, and a bullet fired from that gun had been removed from Skagen's shoulder. Moreover, Richardson himself had freely confessed to the possession of the gun, and admitted that he had fired it. All told, there was ample evidence to prove that Richardson was guilty of "Possession of a Weapon as a Felony," the sixth count of the indictment.

The fifth count of the indictment, charging "Reckless Endangerment in the Second Degree," also posed no serious problems. Its proof turned on the confrontation on Bruckner Boulevard between Richardson and Patrolman Jacobsen. According to Jacobsen, Richardson had pointed his gun at Jacobsen in the course of their struggle. With only four rounds fired, the gun still had one live round in it. Although it did not go off, it might well have, and the action was a reckless act that had endangered Jacobsen's safety.

The fourth count of the indictment, charging "Escape in the Second Degree," posed much greater problems. To commit an escape, in the legal sense of the word, Richardson first had to be lawfully under arrest. In addition, to raise the crime to the level of Escape in the Second Degree, the defendant had to be under arrest for a felony. Was Richardson lawfully under arrest in the Hunts Point subway station, and if so, was he under arrest for a felony?

To answer these questions, I reasoned that at the moment he complied with Skagen's demand and placed his hands against the wall because a gun was pointed at him, Richardson was in custody. On or off duty, John Skagen was a police officer with a sworn obligation to carry a gun and keep the peace. Taking Richardson into custody constituted an arrest.

No one could be certain of Skagen's motive or motives for arresting Richardson. However, the most reasonable argument seemed to be that he had stopped the defendant because he saw the gun tucked in his belt. Why else would an off-duty cop, tired from a long day's work and eager to get home to his wife and dinner, arrest a total stranger? Only something as serious as a gun could prompt such a response. Furthermore, it was Richardson's own explanation for his arrest. I accepted this explanation, and made it part of my argument.

As I saw it, Skagen had arrested Richardson, even if only for a minute, for the felonious possession of a pistol. The rest was easy. Richardson had gotten away from Patrolman Skagen and taken flight. That constituted an escape.

This left the three homicide charges, "Murder," "Attempted Murder" and "Reckless Manslaughter." These charges were far more grave than the other four and presented a far more serious legal problem. I started with Murder, the first count.

The law of New York State actually recognizes three separate crimes that it labels "Murder." The first of these, common-law or intentional murder, is a crime in which an individual, with the unlawful intent to do so, causes the death of another person or of some third person. This crime is a deliberate or intentional one, but it is not necessarily (contrary to common belief) a premeditated crime. To prove common-law murder, it would be necessary to show that Richardson had actually intended to kill Skagen. In returning its indictment against Richardson, the grand jury had not chosen to charge him with common-law murder.

The second form of murder is known as reckless murder. This is the crime in which an individual "under circumstances evincing a depraved indifference to human life, recklessly engages in conduct which creates a grave risk of death to another person, and thereby causes the death of another person." In other words, this is a crime committed by a psychopath or a terrorist, without specific intent and with total disregard for the safety of others. It is, for instance, the bomb thrown into a crowded theater—a depraved, vicious and targetless act. Richardson was not charged with reckless murder.

Richardson *was* charged with the third form of murder, felony murder. The statute defining it reads as follows:

> A person is guilty of murder when: . . . Acting either alone or with one or more other persons, he commits or attempts to commit . . . escape in the second degree, and, in the course of and in furtherance of such crime or in immediate flight therefrom, he, or another participant, if there be any, causes the death of a person other than one of the participants.

In short, Richardson was charged with killing Skagen during the course of a felonious escape. I did not have to prove that he had intended Skagen's death, or that he had acted with depraved indifference to human life—only that he had brought about Skagen's death in furtherance of his escape.

I had already framed my argument on the legal propriety of the escape count, and was committed to the proposition that Richardson had escaped from Skagen's arrest. I was reasonably confident that this argument would pass muster in the courts. Skagen's death could not be open to question, nor would the fact that he had been fatally injured during the course of the escape. By no stretch of the imagination could he be called a participant in the escape. This left only one question: Could Richardson in any sense be said to have caused Skagen's death?

The most that could be said of the two shoulder wounds directly inflicted by Richardson was that they contributed to the cause of death. However, these wounds had been far less serious than the three abdominal injuries caused by Patrolman Wieber's bullets, and their contribution to the bleeding that caused the death was relatively minor. Nevertheless, those few cases that I could find on the question of multiple injuries causing death (and they were very old cases), indicated that anyone who inflicted even the smallest wound contributing to another's death could be said legally to have caused that death. The medical examiner was prepared to testify that the shoulder wounds were a contributory cause of death. Technically this was all that I needed, notwithstanding the three police-inflicted bullets, to claim that Richardson had caused Skagen's death.

But this was really not enough. The logic of my case was such that I went even further, and advanced the novel argument, based on the facts of this case, that Richardson was criminally responsible for the bullets fired by Patrolman Wieber, as well as for those he fired himself. Simply stated, I contended that Patrolman Wieber was an unwitting "participant" in Richardson's escape attempt. Richardson had known that Skagen was chasing him with his gun drawn, and that he was dressed in civilian clothing. Richardson had seen Patrolman Wieber in uniform at the top of the stairs with his gun drawn, and when he shouted to Wieber, "He's shooting at me! A crazy man is shooting!" he was dishonestly and deceptively inviting Wieber to shoot Skagen. The deception worked. Wieber did shoot, and Skagen's pursuit of Richardson ended tragically. At Richardson's dishonest invitation, Patrolman

Wieber had participated in and aided his escape, and this made Richardson criminally responsible for Wieber's actions.

There was no reported case that I could find, either in the state or federal courts, with a fact pattern like this one. The only example I could find that was roughly analogous was one in which a robbery victim, in an effort to defend himself and thwart the robber, drew a gun and fired at the robber, but inadvertently missed and killed an innocent bystander. In such cases (and they were surprisingly numerous) the question arose as to whether the robber could be charged with the murder of the bystander who had been killed by the victim. Courts in Pennsylvania, California and Texas had all answered this question in the affirmative, and had permitted the robber to stand trial for murder. However, the New York State Court of Appeals, the highest court in the state, in the case of *People* v. *Wood,* had taken the opposite position. Therefore, I had to show that the *Wood* case did not apply to the facts of the Richardson case. In that case the court had based its decision on the wording of the felony murder statute requiring that the killing had to be done by a "participant" in the felony, and not by a victim of it. In *Wood,* the killer had been a victim and not a participant. My position was that in the *Richardson* case Patrolman Wieber had been an *unwitting* and *nonculpable* participant in the defendant's escape. Wieber certainly was not a victim of the escape, and had done nothing to thwart it.

Some legal precedent existed to support my position. For instance, it had long been the law that one person may be criminally responsible for the actions of another if he "solicits, requests, commands, importunes, or intentionally aids . . ." that person to engage in criminal conduct. Even if the one who actually commits the criminal act is not himself guilty of any crime, by reason of his ignorance of the criminal nature of his conduct or of the criminal purposes of the person who persuaded him to act, the person who put him up to it can still be guilty.

For example, if I were to dishonestly tell a friend that I lived at a certain address and gave him a key to that dwelling, asking him to retrieve some valuables of mine that were located there, and if he believed me and innocently brought me these valuables, then my friend would be guilty of no crime. Although his actions actually constituted burglary and larceny, he acted with the honest belief that he was on lawful business. I, on the other hand, would be guilty of both burglary and larceny because I had put my friend up to these acts, knowing full well that they were illegal.

Pushing this hypothetical situation even further, suppose that upon entering the dwelling he mistakenly believes to be mine, my unfortunate friend is attacked by the actual owner of the premises, who believes that my friend is a burglar. Suppose, further, that my friend defends himself, and in so doing kills the true owner of the valuables. My friend, who is innocent of any burglary, and who has killed in self-defense, would still be guilty of no crime. I, however, would be guilty of felony murder, because I had induced and was criminally responsible for my friend's actions.

The Richardson case paralleled this hypothetical one. The defendant deceived Patrolman Wieber, and led him to the erroneous but not unreasonable conclusion that John Skagen was a dangerous criminal in the process of committing a violent crime. Richardson did this with the obvious intention of tangling up the two policemen so that he could escape. The shots Wieber had fired, and which had contributed so substantially to the cause of Skagen's death, unquestionably furthered Richardson's efforts to escape. Thus, Wieber's innocence did not let Richardson off the hook; instead, it made all the more terrible his guilt of murder.

The reckless manslaughter count of the indictment posed many of the same legal problems as the felony murder count. It was the same death, caused in the same fashion, and many of the arguments advanced to support the murder charge were identical with those applicable to that of manslaughter. The only real difference between the two charges lay in the varying mental states charged to the defendant by each count. In the murder count Richardson was charged with the intention of escaping from an arrest, and this intent, leading to the actions that caused the death, was essential to the murder charge. The manslaughter count, on the other hand, was a crime without either motive or intention, and required only a criminally reckless mental state.

A man is reckless when he is aware of, but consciously disregards, the substantial and unjustifiable risk that his actions will cause some unlawful result. Simply stated, firing four pistol shots in a crowded subway station was a grossly reckless act. Richardson knew that firing those shots put the life of everyone in the subway station in danger, but he fired nevertheless. Then, compounding this recklessness, he shouted his fatal words to Patrolman Wieber. Again, Richardson disregarded the almost certain fact that his shout would encourage gunplay from Wieber, and would endanger both Skagen and the civilians in the station. Crying "Fire!" in a crowded public place is the classic textbook example of recklessness. In effect, this is what Richardson had done.

The final count was "Attempted Murder." In a legal and factual sense, this was the easiest count to establish. It turned entirely upon the four shots Richardson had fired at Skagen from close range. My argument was that these shots were convincing proof of Richardson's intent to kill. Why else would one fire four shots at a person? If Richardson had indeed intended to kill Skagen and failed, then he had committed the crime of Attempted Murder. Thus, if either the trial judge, on legal grounds, or the jury, on factual grounds, were unwilling to accept my arguments about Richardson's criminal responsibility for causing Skagen's death, I would have the attempted murder count to fall back on. Being an "attempt" charge, I did not have to prove Skagen's death at all, let alone what caused it.

Putting together these and similar legal arguments was the sort of thing that I had been taught at Columbia Law School. Digging through the law books, finding obscure legal precedents and playing an advocate's role in an intellectual sphere was a refreshing relief from the grim realities of homicide prosecution. For better or for worse, I was ready to argue law with Kunstler, but I was aware of and respected the fact that he had once taught law. I was looking forward to the legal arguments. In fact, the more prepared I became, the more eager I was for the trial to begin.

18

Negotiating a Plea

There came a time to step back from the preparations. The witnesses were ready to testify, and the charts, diagrams, models, photographs, documents and physical evidence had all been assembled. Experts and technicians had been consulted, and had offered their opinions. The legal research was done, and a memorandum of law prepared. I believed that I knew the Richardson case as well as it could be known. I was ready to try the case, ready to win it.

This emphasis on "winning" or "losing" is reflective of a trial lawyer's task. Litigators are deliberately cast in an adversarial role, and prepare their cases knowing that the ultimate trial is a winner-take-all contest. Trial lawyers are said to win or lose their cases, and reputations are made or lost accordingly. Cases are prepared with this in mind. Within the obvious constraints of presenting only truthful witnesses, concealing no exculpatory evidence and honoring the rules of evidence and procedure, a trial lawyer will do everything within his power to obtain a favorable verdict. In court he neither gives nor asks for quarter, and the tasks of being neutral, of dispassionately evaluating the evidence and of arriving at a just verdict are left to the judge and jury. Trial lawyers are like athletes: they compete, and they win or they lose.

I expected to win, but I was also prepared for the possibility of losing. Just the same, before the time came to begin, I had to reflect on the Richardson case and evaluate it not as a contest to be won but as a matter to be justly resolved. I sat up for a few nights with my wife, talking about the case. I tried to resolve in my mind just how bad Richardson's actions really had been, and just what punishment, if any, he really deserved. These were not easy questions.

In truth, there is a tremendous ambivalence—almost a schizophrenia—that the quasi-judicial role of a prosecutor imposes upon an assistant district attorney. On the one hand, he is a trial advocate, expected to do everything in his power to obtain convictions. On the other hand, he is sworn to administer justice dispassionately, to seek humane dispositions rather than to blindly extract every last drop of punishment from every case. There is a tension that exists between the desire to "win" every case and the desire to do the right thing in each particular one. Such tension does not always exist, for there are cases where harshness is called for. But all too often the two goals of justice and victory are not totally compatible. Whenever this happens, the desire for victory should give way to the desire for justice. However, for an ambitious and aggressive trial lawyer this is easier said than done, and during such cases the tension never subsides.

Technically, according to the facts as I knew them and the law as I understood it, Richardson was guilty of the murder of a police officer. There is no crime in the entire penal law that has traditionally been viewed with more horror than the murder of a police officer, and it is a crime that is punished severely. In June of 1972 the murder of a policeman was punishable by death in New York State. If tried promptly and convicted of murder, James Richardson might have been electrocuted.

But by the time I began to prepare the Richardson case, the Supreme Court of the United States, in the case of *Furman* v. *Georgia,* had outlawed all existing capital punishment statutes as unconstitutional. Although the New York State Legislature would later pass a new statute reinstating the death penalty for the murder of a policeman, as far as the Richardson case was concerned, the *Furman* decision was binding, and he could not be sentenced to death. He did face a possible life sentence, however, and in many ways this was a prospect even more terrible than electrocution. To be locked in a jail cell day after day, year after year, shut off from all normal human contact, without hope of release, is a form of psychic suffering almost impossible to comprehend. I did not believe that justice demanded that James Richardson should receive a life sentence. There were many murderers I had prosecuted who were far more vicious than he was. I had been involved with cases of murder for hire—of men who for a fee would cold-bloodedly take the life of a total stranger. There were cases of hardened robbers who, after having taken their money, had calmly slaughtered shopkeepers so that there would be no witnesses. There was one case of a man who had raped and then drowned a nine-year-old girl. Compared to any of these, the Richardson case diminished in gravity, and in this perspective he did not deserve the most extreme punishment envisioned by law.

In fairness, Richardson's crime had been a spur-of-the-moment affair. There was no premeditated malice involved—rather, an on-the-spot desperation to avoid arrest and possible imprisonment. Moreover, in spite of his prior record, Richardson was neither a hardened criminal nor a "cop killer" in the usual sense of the phrase. Caught up abruptly in a situation, in a way he was as much a victim of circumstances as he was the perpetrator of a crime. It was not imperative that he be convicted of murder and sentenced to life imprisonment.

Still, I could not bring myself to accept the extreme opposite view of the case, either. I certainly could not persuade myself that Richardson should be released outright, without any further punishment for the crimes he had committed. On the afternoon of June 28, 1972, he had taken a human life, and his acts, desperate and unpremeditated though they may have been, were those of a dangerous and reckless man. He had been a fugitive from justice, he was carrying a concealed deadly weapon, and he displayed a frightening readiness to use it on a stranger he knew to be a police officer.

In addition, Richardson's background, to the extent that it could be judged, did not reveal him to be a good man. He was not so bad as many, but he was a man who displayed a marked disrespect for the law and for the well-being of his fellow man. I felt that he deserved to be punished.

In the abstract, these thoughts were all well and good. I could endlessly debate the philosophical pros and cons of crime and punishment as they applied to James Richardson. But sooner or later reality had to be faced; I had to come up with a number rather than a philosophy. How many years did I feel that Richardson should spend in prison for his deeds?

I knew of no equation that would automatically answer this question, and there was nothing scientific about my thought processes. My judgment in the matter was largely intuitive, and I could not begin to articulate adequately how I finally arrived at a number: twelve years.

I knew perfectly well that twelve years in jail—or twelve days—would serve no useful purpose. Prison was not going to rehabilitate Richardson; if anything, it would make his behavior even more uncivilized. I also did not believe that sentencing him to a lengthy prison term would have any deterrent effect upon others. Human motivation, and particularly the motivation to commit crime, is far too complex a phenomenon to be easily encouraged or discouraged. Besides, the facts of the Richardson case were so unusual that there was no real reason to expect them to occur again, and therefore no real reason to try to deter future James Richardsons.

Having rejected the two old prosecutorial chestnuts of

rehabilitation and deterrence, I was primarily motivated by two thoughts. First, I felt that society deserved to be protected from the future acts of James Richardson himself. He seemed a dangerous and violent man, and there was no reason why the people of New York City should be subjected to the probability of his future violence. If he were permitted to go free after what he had done, there was every reason to believe that eventually he would hurt some other innocent person.

My second thought was frankly one of retribution. Richardson had taken a human life and had brought untold suffering to the John Skagen family. Admittedly, no punishment could ever undo what he had done, but the failure to punish Richardson severely would undeniably be a terrible injustice to the memory of John Skagen. Vengeance and retribution may not be pretty sentiments, but they are very real psychological needs, and the law—and indeed even our major religions—recognize this fact. Even a few minutes spent talking to Pat Skagen brought this truth home. In some raw, almost primordial sense, justice demanded that Richardson be punished.

Why twelve years? Other people in the district attorney's office with whom I discussed the matter suggested other numbers. By and large, the sentiment in the office was for a much harsher sentence. But one man agreed with me, and he was the person who counted. Mario Merola, the district attorney who had succeeded Burton Roberts in January 1973, accepted my arguments. Merola, an essentially fair and humane man, authorized me to seek a disposition. His words of advice to me, plain and simple, were, "Go ahead and do the right thing. Don't worry about any criticism, and do what you have to do. I'll back you up."

Armed with these assurances, I got in touch with Kunstler. I set out to see if a guilty plea could be negotiated.

Negotiating guilty pleas, or plea bargaining, is the great safety valve, the only factor that stands between the criminal justice system and utter chaos. For without this practice, every defendant charged with an offense, however grave or trivial, would have to go to trial; and if every case were tried, with existing resources, a man arrested today would have to wait twenty-five years for his case to come up. At the present time roughly 95 percent of those charged with crimes in New York City plead guilty rather than go to trial.

Simply stated, plea bargaining is that practice in which a defendant waives his right to trial by jury, and in open court admits his guilt to a charge that has been leveled against him. In return for this admission, the court and the prosecution generally agree to permit that defendant to plead guilty to a less serious charge than the one that he faces (e.g., trespassing rather than burglary, or manslaughter rather than murder), and promise him a lighter sentence than the one he would receive if convicted after trial of the higher charge.

The great "virtue" of plea bargaining for both the defense and the prosecution is that it eliminates uncertainty. A defendant charged with murder, for instance, by "copping a plea" can generally eliminate the possibility of a life sentence, or in some cases even electrocution. The prosecution, on the other hand, by recommending the acceptance of a plea eliminates the possibility of seeing a bad criminal go free because of some real or imagined weakness in its case. As in all important human matters, there is a strong disinclination to gamble, and both sides, in effect, opt for a sure thing.

The abuses caused by plea bargaining are many and manifest. To begin with—and clearly this is the worst abuse—there are individuals innocent of any offense who plead guilty rather than face the possible consequences of an adverse verdict. An innocent man, caught in a web of circumstances that make him appear guilty—for instance, a misidentified defendant—may well think it wiser to plead guilty and take a certain five-year sentence rather than run the risk that a jury might believe the mistaken victim, convict him, and subject him to a twenty-five-year sentence.

There is no way of knowing how many innocent men have

pleaded guilty over the years, but it clearly has happened many times. Certainly, no decent prosecutor or judge would knowingly recommend or accept a guilty plea from an innocent individual. However, without benefit of a trial, and without ample time to conduct an investigation, there is no real way for either judges or prosecutors with their crushing dockets and caseloads to form much of an opinion on guilt or innocence. The available information is almost always sketchy and incomplete, and both time and resources are lacking for it to be otherwise. Once a plea is taken, there is no further review of the merits of a case.

Plea bargaining discourages trials by rewarding those who plead guilty with markedly light punishment. The fiction which justifies this practice is the idea that by pleading guilty a man displays remorse for his deeds, and that this remorse is the first step on the road to repentance and rehabilitation. This supposed display of repentance in turn is said to justify lenient treatment.

In fact, the sole justification for plea bargaining is expediency and nothing else. The practice actually penalizes those defendants who assert their constitutional right to trial by jury, for those who demand a trial and then lose are bound to receive the harshest sentences. They receive these sentences not because they are more guilty than those who plead, and not because they are more deserving of punishment than those who plead, but because they have had the audacity to demand their rights, and in the process have taken up a big chunk of the court's and prosecutor's limited time.

Another abuse of the plea-bargaining system is the near-universal practice of overcharging defendants. Prosecutors, knowing full well that they will have to bargain down in order to dispose of their cases, strain and stretch the law so as to charge a defendant with the highest possible crime. By inflating the charges, often beyond the true scope of the available evidence, they improve their bargaining position immensely. If a case is evaluated as being "worth" five years, the chances are that a defendant will find himself charged with a crime that carries with it a twenty-five-year sentence. Ultimately the prosecutor permits himself to be "talked into" the reduction to a five-year sentence.

Plea bargaining encourages delay. The very concept of bargaining suggests an ongoing negotiation, and in practice both sides are always willing to delay if they sense that a better deal might be obtained in the future. Negotiation implies give-and-take, and give-and-take requires time. Time means delay, and in criminal justice delay is very bad. The innocent suffer and the guilty benefit.

Plea bargaining also gives too much unsupervised power to prosecutors. Knowing full well that the odds are twenty to one against any given case going to trial, prosecutors can afford to be sloppy or even vindictive in initiating cases. In the vast majority of cases neither judges nor juries get to review the merits of the prosecution. It is not unheard-of for prosecutors to bring indictments against people whom they believe to be guilty, even though they have insufficient evidence to legally prove guilt. The theory is that a plea can always be obtained long before the inadequate case must be tried; as a result there is little likelihood of embarrassment. Plea bargaining can turn a prosecutor, especially if he is lazy or unscrupulous, into both judge and jury.

We are condemned to plea bargaining by society's indifference. The Richardson case turned out to be a rare exception to the norm, in that an enormous amount of time and effort was expended in arriving at an ultimate disposition. It was the one case in a hundred that everyone always assumed would have to be tried, and it was prepared accordingly. Nevertheless, to understand the Richardson case you must understand the system in which it occurred—and to understand that system you must understand plea bargaining.

*   *   *

It took a couple of weeks to even get an appointment with Kunstler. His long-suffering but good-natured secretary made excuse after excuse for his inability to find the time to discuss the case. I didn't press the issue because I didn't want to seem too eager. I was concerned that such an attitude might be misinterpreted as either fear or weakness, and I knew that if Kunstler thought my case had holes in it, there would be no plea bargain.

In time Kunstler did make the trip to Bronx County to discuss the case. We shook hands, and I ushered him into my cubicle. I was prepared to be deferential to an older and far more famous attorney, but he immediately put our discussions on a "Bill" and "Steve" basis.

"Steve, you know, it's going to be a pleasure to try a case in Bronx County again. I used to try cases up here years ago. I don't think I've ever lost one up here."

He was confident and relaxed. I brought us down to business and started to talk about the Richardson case. I told him of my preparations, and gave him copies of the police reports and all the rest of the documentary evidence. I took great pains to explain the facts of my case as I saw them, and to make clear to him that I intended to prove them. I had no desire to try to surprise Kunstler in the courtroom; instead, I wanted him to understand and acknowledge the fact that there was a serious, even a compelling case against his client.

I failed. Right up until the moment of verdict, Kunstler never evidenced the slightest appreciation of the serious danger his client was in. Perhaps this was a pose; I simply don't know. Perhaps it was his sincere evaluation of the case. "Steve," he said to me, "You're never going to get a jury to convict Richardson on those facts. Oh, maybe you'll get them to go for the stolen badge, but nothing else. Face reality."

Our conversation drifted, and we started to talk about the criminal justice system. I began to try to explain to him about both the problems and the rewards of being a prosecutor, and of what I had hoped to accomplish in becoming an assistant district attorney. I expressed my deep admiration for what I thought he had been doing, and our talk became cordial. We philosophized. Kunstler speculated about the possibility of his being a prosecutor one day. It was an interesting thought. It still is.

I was seeking common ground that I knew we could agree upon. I talked of my disgust with the prison system, and of my unhappiness with the way Rockefeller had handled the Attica riots. I agreed with his assertion that prison would not do Richardson any good. Slowly, warily, we began to inch toward the heart of the matter. Our talk had been polite, even cordial, but so far it had been no more than an intellectual ballet, a cautious mutual exploration.

When I told Kunstler that I felt no need to convict Richardson of murder, he abruptly told me that Richardson was prepared to plead guilty if an acceptable bargain could be reached. I kept my outward composure, but inwardly I was stunned. It had come so casually. Kunstler was prepared to plead Richardson guilty! There would be no trial. For a moment I really believed that there might be a fair disposition amicably arrived at.

Then Kunstler added, "Under no circumstance, of course, will I permit Richardson to take a plea if he is to get jail time I will not let him go to jail."

That was that. I told Kunstler that we could only accept a plea bargain that carried with it substantial jail time. I did not even attempt to explain why I felt this way; there was no point. I knew that I could not persuade him to change his attitude, and that he could not alter mine. Now that a trial was inevitable, I wished to keep our relationship on the most cordial basis possible. It seemed more prudent to agree about mutual beliefs than to debate our differences.

Eventually we had a meeting with Merola, during which Kunstler reiterated his insistence upon no jail sentence. Merola listened courteously and refused.

19

On the Eve of Trial

The summer of 1974 came and went. Wounded Knee limped on its seemingly endless way toward a verdict, and with my preparations completed there was nothing for me to do but turn my attentions to other, unrelated cases. Before the Richardson case actually went to trial, I prepared, tried and obtained convictions in two other murder cases. Through it all, each week without fail Pat Skagen would call, and each week I had to offer her the same excuses and explanations. I came to dread her calls.

In September, Wounded Knee went to a jury and at long last Kunstler was free—or, at least, nearly free—to try the Richardson case. As it turned out, prosecutors all over the country had been waiting for Kunstler to become free. It seemed that there were a dozen cases, each of them major, that had grown old awaiting Kunstler's availability. In particular, the prosecutions growing out of the Attica prison uprising had been so delayed. A judge in Buffalo, New York, where that trial was scheduled to take place, was eager to have Kunstler present in his courtroom. The Attica trial had been delayed even longer than the Richardson case, and for a while it appeared that Kunstler would go directly to Buffalo and begin a trial there that could (and in fact, did) take months to complete. It was a horrifying prospect.

Fate, in the guise of Ramsey Clark's nomination as the Democratic candidate for the United States Senate in New York State, intervened. Clark was Kunstler's co-counsel in the Attica case, so when he was nominated the decision was made in Buffalo to put off the Attica trial until November. This freed Kunstler to try the Richardson case in the interim. In retrospect, it was to be a relatively obscure and brief interlude for him between two celebrated cases, Wounded Knee and Attica.

A trial judge had to be assigned to the Richardson case. At that time in the Bronx there were five judges presiding over homicide cases, and trials were assigned to their parts on a more or less random basis. The assignments themselves were made by Justice William Kappelman, the deputy chief administrative judge for Bronx County, and he himself was one of these five judges. He could not take the trial himself for the simple reason that he was disqualified from doing so because Bill Quinn, the assistant district attorney who had originally presented the case to the grand jury, had become his legal secretary. Eventually I was informed that the case had been sent to the trial part of Justice Ivan Warner, and that he would preside.

Though some had predicted otherwise at the time of his election to the State Supreme Court, Ivan Warner turned out to be one of the finest trial jurists in Bronx County. He had been a state senator before his ascension to the bench, and it was feared that even as a judge he would be more a practicing politician than a legal scholar. However, Justice Warner's greatest virtue as a jurist turned out to be his willingness to go to the lawbooks and to carefully research any legal problem that came before him. Many judges, feeling supreme in their own courtrooms, have a tendency to shoot from the hip and to make on-the-spot rulings on even the most complex and subtle legal problems. But from the outset Justice Warner displayed an appetite for legal research and a willingness to listen to the legal arguments of counsel. In a case with the enormous complexities of *People* v. *Richardson*, it was a relief to have a judge who would pay careful attention to the legal issues raised.

Many judges develop reputations for being defense- or prosecution-oriented. Justice Warner is known as being right down the middle, and both the assistant district attorneys and the defense bar of Bronx County generally agree that they get a fair trial in his courtroom. He is scrupulously impartial, and has never been accused—as some judges have been—of intervening in a trial to influence a jury. He is also a no-nonsense judge. Young and vigorous by all judicial standards, he is on the bench at 9:30 A.M. and does not like to adjourn court until 5:00 P.M. During the trial, he would exasperate me with his constant admonitions that my witnesses be always available outside the courtroom, so that when one finished testifying, another would be ready to begin immediately. He insists upon setting a rapid pace in his trials, and is impatient with delay, taking the position that it is better to place some strain upon counsel than to waste the time of the judge and jury.

Justice Warner runs a very tight courtroom. A stickler for decorum, he will not tolerate improper antics from attorneys, defendants, witnesses or the audience. He is a strong judge who is well suited to deal with a flamboyant or difficult attorney, and when I learned that he was to preside over the Richardson case, I was interested to see how he would react to Kunstler.

Though he has a reputation for fairness, Justice Warner also is widely known as a tough judge. The word is that while you get a fair trial from him, Lord help you if you are convicted, because he will throw the book at you. He has a well-developed philosophy of punishing wrongdoing severely, and of protect-

ing the citizens of Bronx County whom he has so long repre-
sented. Ivan Warner has never lost sight of the victims in the
cases that come before him, and by no stretch of the imagination can he be called a "bleeding heart."

Perhaps one other factor should be mentioned about Ivan
Warner. Strictly speaking, this should have no effect upon
evaluating the role that he would play in the Richardson case,
but realistically it cannot be ignored. Ivan Warner is a black
man.

At the time the Richardson case was moved to trial, I had
appeared before Justice Warner only once before. I did not
really know him well, and, of course, I did not expect him to
know Kunstler save by reputation. To my surprise, on the first
day of the trial when Kunstler entered the courtroom, the
judge smiled at him and said, "Hi, Prof." I quickly learned that
many years before, Kunstler had taught Warner at law school.
At first this revelation disturbed me, but it soon became clear
that the relationship in no way affected the judge's rulings. He
gave both sides a fair trial.

20

A Search for the Truth

In theory, a trial by jury is a search for the truth. In practice, it is a great deal more. There are many values and forces, sometimes in conflict and sometimes in harmony, that combine to make up a jury trial. The search for truth is only one of them. There is nothing simple about trial by jury.

For instance, by constitutional fiat jury trials must protect individuals against self-incrimination, unlawful search and seizure, and a host of other possible governmental abuses. Trial by one's peers is nothing if not a safeguard against arbitrary or excessive governmental action.

However, in a totally different but no less real sense, trial by jury is a contest between attorneys. In every trial one lawyer must emerge the winner, and the other the loser. This adversarial competition is approved and encouraged, and in the end this sense of competition permeates and even affects the outcome of trials, often quite independently of all other considerations. A trial is a contest as well as an ordeal.

A jury trial is also a drama, a performance in which roles

are imposed upon individuals. The demands of these imposed roles generally assume a life of their own, often above and beyond the intentions of the individual actors. In trial by jury life imitates art; it is living theater. It is also politics, in both the noblest and the basest senses of the word. A criminal trial is an almost primordial confrontation between the individual and society. At stake are values no less important than individual liberty on the one hand, and the need for social order on the other. It is also pragmatic, grass-roots clubhouse politics in its rawest form. Trial by jury is publicity, the news media, and the making and unmaking of reputations. Many a political career has begun or ended in a criminal courtroom.

Lastly, trial by jury is life in microcosm, an amalgam of many diverse values that are only imperfectly resolved. It is endlessly complex and endlessly fascinating. In short, it is much more than a search for the truth—and much less.

A trial culminates in a "verdict," a word of Latin origin which means to speak the truth. By social and legal convention, it is accepted that juries discover and then pronounce the truth. Implicitly assumed by this convention is that somewhere there is a truth that can be discovered. Is it an objective or a subjective phenomenon? Does it depend upon the particular viewpoint of the individual who seeks it? When can something be said to be true?

These are not easily answered questions. Debates about truth have raged in philosophical circles for millennia, and no doubt will continue to do so indefinitely. It is certainly not my intention in the scope of this book to venture an answer to these questions. For present purposes, it is enough to acknowledge their existence and to leave their answers to the philosophers. Of course, we all share a more or less common understanding of what is meant by speaking the truth, and we all know what it is to lie. Philosophical uncertainty has never stopped mankind from routinely judging things to be true or false. Logic, experience, intuition and emotion all combine to permit such judgments. In one way or another, most people are able to agree upon truth and its opposite, and for the purposes of a criminal trial that is enough.

If permitted, juries would find facts in much the same way that, as individuals, they make important decisions. All available information would be evaluated in the light of experience. Opinions would be solicited, and even such intangibles as rumor and general speculation might be considered. Only then would a determination be reached.

In fact this is not what happens. During jury trials, important and even crucial facts are often kept from the jury. This is not done for sinister reasons; on the contrary, only the most compelling and worthwhile values such as the protection of individual rights can justify keeping facts from a jury. Nevertheless, there are times when the search for truth is subordinated to other values.

I once tried a case of armed robbery in which the defendant had been arrested one day after the robbery with the proceeds of the theft in his possession. He had robbed a sporting-goods store, and had taken a number of hunting rifles. The following day, while driving in a different neighborhood (perhaps looking for another store to rob), he had been stopped by a suspicious police officer, who asked for his driver's license and registration. When the driver failed to produce these documents, the officer arrested him, searched the automobile, and found the stolen rifles. Later, the robber was picked out of a line-up by the victims of the robbery.

At the very outset of the trial, the defense attorney moved to suppress the evidence of the rifles on the ground that they were seized as a result of an unconstitutional search. A hearing was held; the trial judge ruled that the police officer's search was indeed unconstitutional and ordered that the rifles be excluded from evidence. This meant that the jury would never learn that the rifles were recovered, and that they had been in the possession of the defendant. My case was seriously weakened by this ruling.

The police officer who had arrested the defendant had not acted in bad faith. He had truly believed that he was entitled to search the man's car, and his belief had not been unreasonable. The law governing the propriety of warrantless searches of automobiles has been uncertain even at the appellate level in recent years. However, the officer's mistake did not change the fact that the defendant had possession of the stolen rifles only one day after the robbery. This fact, especially when coupled with the positive identification of the defendant by the victims, was powerful proof of his guilt. The fact of possession did not become any less true because of the unconstitutional nature of the search that revealed it.

At the trial the defense attorney actually argued to the jury that the prosecution's failure to produce the stolen rifles entitled the defendant to an acquittal. So far as the jury ever learned, the rifles were never recovered. As it turned out, the robber was convicted anyway. The suppression of evidence did not make a difference because the jury chose to believe the testimony of the victims. They might not have done so, however, and suppressed evidence frequently makes all the difference in the world in determining the outcome of a jury trial.

Still, I have no quarrel with the exclusionary rule. There are times when the prevention of police abuse, of unlawful searches and coerced confessions, is more important than the search for truth. I would sooner see some guilty men go free than live in a society where police abuse goes unchecked. There are times during a jury trial when the truth must be suppressed in the name of the Bill of Rights.

The Constitution is not the only document that limits a free search for information. Legal rules of evidence often prevent juries from learning crucial facts. There is often a great difference between what an attorney knows to be true and what he may attempt to prove in court.

For instance, much of what we learn on this earth is gained

secondhand. Some things we see or hear directly and learn from our senses; most of what we learn, however, comes from teachers, the printed word, television and just plain word of mouth. Such evidence is known as hearsay, and generally it is not admitted into evidence at a trial, even though we routinely rely upon such information in our daily affairs. The courts have decreed that hearsay evidence is often unreliable and should not be trusted. However, as any psychologist will readily admit, eyewitness identification of strangers is also extremely unreliable. Nevertheless, such identification is invariably submitted to juries for evaluation, whereas hearsay evidence is rarely even considered. Word of mouth and "the grapevine" are invaluable to the investigator; they are worthless to the trial lawyer.

Trial procedures can also conflict with the free search for the truth. One such procedure is the rule that only the attorneys (and, very rarely, the trial judge) are able to ask questions of the witnesses. The twelve individuals in the jury who must ultimately speak the truth in their verdict must be mute at all other times. Either individually or collectively, the jurors cannot ask questions; all they are permitted to do is listen.

The problems created by this procedure were brought home to me in one of the first cases I ever tried, a robbery case in which my witnesses, a barkeeper and his daughter, had identified the man who had robbed them. They were both strong, sympathetic witnesses; their testimony was persuasive and powerful and I expected the jury to return a quick conviction. To my surprise, it took two full days of deliberation for the jury to return a guilty verdict. I couldn't imagine what had given the panel such a problem, and I spent the two days trying to figure which juror was unreasonably holding out.

After the trial ended I learned what had concerned the jury. I had been dead wrong in blaming a holdout; the jury had spent its time carefully debating an issue that both the defense attorney and I had overlooked.

During the testimony, both the barkeeper and his daughter

had described the robber as wearing a hat, and I had neglected to ask either of them to describe it. The defense attorney never inquired about it in his cross-examination, either, and in our summations neither of us referred to it.

In their deliberations, however, a number of jurors became concerned about this hat. It was reasoned that a wide-brimmed hat could have hidden the robber's features and cast doubt upon my witnesses' identification. In point of fact, the hat in question was a beanie, and would not have disguised the robber. But the jury had no way of knowing this, and it disturbed them. Had they been given the opportunity to question the witnesses, one of the jurors undoubtedly would have sought a description of the hat, and the answer would have made their deliberations easier. In some cases, such questions can make the difference between a guilty verdict and an acquittal.

There is no reason why trial procedures should not be altered to allow jurors to question witnesses. They could put their questions in writing to the trial judge, who could rule on the questions' legal propriety, and then ask them himself. Such a method is not unlike practices currently followed by American grand juries, and in the trial courts of some European nations.

The metaphor may be imperfect, but there is no question that in many ways a criminal trial resembles a play, and that a trial lawyer's role closely resembles that of the director. The director has the playwright's script; the attorney has the facts revealed by his investigation. The director has his cast of actors; the lawyer has his group of witnesses. Both director and attorney try to make the most of the material available and put together the best possible presentation.

Plays are directed at drama critics and at the playgoing public; trials seek to win over juries, the news media and the general public. Both plays and trials have distinct audiences whom they seek to persuade. Credibility or verisimilitude are extremely important both in the theater and in the courtroom. A jury trial is a performance, no question about it. The judge, jury, defendant, attorneys and witnesses all have roles to play —and all are conscious of this. The approaches to each role may differ from individual to individual, but regardless of how natural a person may seem in a courtroom, you can be certain that he is putting on something of an act. Nobody that I've ever met acts the same in a courtroom as he does outside it.

Obviously, the rules of good drama and the demands of truth are not always the same. Truth is often stranger than fiction, but a good trial lawyer must never permit his case to seem implausible. He must make it appear to be true. Still, truth and the *appearance* of truth are not necessarily the same thing.

The idea of trial by jury as competition has already been mentioned, and its importance cannot be overemphasized. We are committed to an adversarial system of criminal justice. Competition is not only sanctioned in the courtroom, it is applauded. Attorneys are expected to be partisan in approach; within broad constraints they are supposed to slant every fact to assist their client's case. Sometimes truth will suffer in the give-and-take of competition.

Even a guilty man is entitled to a vigorous defense. It is quite proper for a defendant to tell his attorney, "I did it, but I want you to defend me because I do not believe the district attorney can prove it." Under such circumstances, a defense attorney has an obligation to try his best to discredit prosecution witnesses, even though he may know them to be truthful. Imagine an old man with weak eyesight and a failing memory who was the victim of a robbery. He identifies the defendant, who has just privately confessed to his attorney. It is a relatively easy matter for a skilled defense attorney to rip the old man's testimony to shreds, casting grave doubts upon his credibility. He must do this even though he knows that the old man is telling the truth, for he is an advocate and his role is to obtain an acquittal for his client, not to search for the truth. To be sure, a defense lawyer may not mount a dishonest defense; he should not call defense witnesses who he knows will lie. Aside from that, his only obligation is to his client.

In medieval Europe there was once a tradition of trial by combat. When two parties had a dispute, each would hire a champion skilled in the martial arts, and these warriors would fight. The party whose champion emerged victorious was deemed to have won the argument. Even today a mystique exists about trial lawyers which is not far removed from the tradition of trial by combat. Instead of a battle with swords and shields fought on an open field, there is verbal combat between two champions, with the victory going to the more persuasive lawyer. In the popular view, it is the side with the "better" lawyer which always wins the case.

This mystique is extremely powerful—and it is also antithetic to the ideals of truth and justice. An individual ought to be either guilty or not guilty, and the proof against him ought to be either sufficient or insufficient to obtain a conviction. A guilty man should not be acquitted because he is ineptly prosecuted and ably defended; conversely, an innocent man should not be convicted because he was brilliantly prosecuted and poorly defended. A jury's verdict ought to reflect the objective truth of the matter in dispute, not the relative skills of the competing attorneys.

Is there any truth to the mystique? Do trial lawyers make a difference in the outcome of a jury trial? The answer is yes, but not nearly to the extent that most lawyers would like to think. In the vast majority of cases even the most able or inept attorney would not make a difference. I have prosecuted cases so powerful, where my evidence was so overwhelming, that I do not believe that Clarence Darrow himself could have successfully defended the case. I have seen other cases so weak that no prosecutor could reasonably have expected to obtain a conviction. In such cases, lawyers and their skills do not make a difference; the facts are too compelling one way or the other. It is only in the close trials that the relative skill of the opposing lawyers becomes truly important. The majority of cases that I have observed have been relatively clear-cut. It is perhaps only in one case in four that a lawyer's skills can hope to affect the outcome. In the rest, the verdict is more or less foreordained by the available evidence. This is something that trial lawyers do not like to admit. There is a great deal of ego that goes into the makeup of such men, and they prefer to take credit for their courtroom "victories" and to think that their talent was responsible for a happy outcome. Most lawyers keep careful track of their "wins" and "losses," and are themselves the worst victims of the mystique that exists about their skills.

Whether or not the *Richardson* case was one of the close cases or one of the majority of cases with a foreordained outcome, I cannot judge.

21

Dress Rehearsal

The first step of most jury trials is evidentiary hearings. They are conducted in front of the trial judge before the jury is selected. The judge presides over the hearings as both a finder of fact and a finder of law; in effect he is the jury as well as the judge.

Generally there are three purposes for holding these pre-trial hearings. The first is to determine whether any physical evidence which the prosecution intends to offer in evidence is the product of unlawful search and seizure. The second is to determine whether any in-court identification of the defendant as the perpetrator of a crime was tainted by a suggestive pre-trial identification procedure—for example, a bad line-up. Lastly, a pre-trial hearing can determine whether any confession obtained by the prosecution was coerced or given freely. If the judge determines, as a matter of fact and law, that physical evidence, identifications or confessions were unlawfully obtained, he will order them suppressed, and the jury will never learn of such evidence.

The only pre-trial hearing necessary in the Richardson case was what has been called in New York State a Huntley Hearing, after the leading case of *People* v. *Huntley*. It was concerned with the legal propriety of any confessions obtained by the prosecution. In this case, Kunstler specifically challenged the statements made by Richardson on the night of June 13, 1972, at Lincoln Hospital, claiming in formal motion papers that they were unlawful.

There were actually seven "confessions" in all. Richardson had made one statement to Patrolman Santiago, two to Detective Cruz, one to Detective Gest, and one to Assistant District Attorney DuBoff. In addition, he had made two statements to civilians: one to Miss Johnson, the admissions clerk, and the other to Blondell Gimbell, his cousin.

Kunstler contended that all seven statements were unlawfully coerced, asserting that Richardson had not been properly advised of his rights. As a fall-back position, he also argued that Richardson had been in such pain that night that he could not possibly have understood his rights or intelligently waived them. Of course I took the opposite position.

Before the hearing began, Kunstler made an interesting application to the court. He asked Justice Warner to designate him, pursuant to section 18(b) of the County Law, as James Richardson's court-appointed attorney. In short, he wanted the State of New York to pay him to represent Richardson.

MR. KUNSTLER: Judge, before the hearing begins, I wanted to [ask] the Court . . . [to appoint me as Richardson's attorney]. Mr. Richardson has no assets whatsoever, except the salary he lives on, and he has been trying to make up ten months debts which he had when he was in jail and received no salary.

[I have frequently applied for such appointment, and it has always been granted. The last time in Bronx County was by Justice Asch in *People* v. *Feliciano*. There has been no objection from the Appellate Division as to such appointments, and they honor all of them.]

THE COURT: What is his occupation?

MR. KUNSTLER: He is an admitting clerk at Lincoln Hospital and he is here to inform Your Honor as to his assets. He has nothing except his salary. He has no bank accounts, no stocks, no car. He supports a large number of children—I think over five—and for ten months he was in jail and could not even put up a nickel of his own. That was all done by friends and supporters at Lincoln Hospital. He has literally no funds to pay for anything. I have not charged him. I told him I would apply to the Court. . .

THE COURT: Have you been retained up to now?

MR. KUNSTLER: Well, I have appeared for him [with] no formal retainer . . . I have never charged him and don't intend to charge him. He has nothing to pay me with, but I have appeared . . . for the last two years for him in one way or another . . .

THE COURT: All right, you are appointed pursuant to 18(b) of the County Law.

MR. KUNSTLER: Thank you, Judge.

I stood silent during Kunstler's application and took no position on the question. As a member of the district attorney's staff it was a matter of indifference to me who paid Kunstler to represent Richardson—or indeed, whether he was paid at all. The state undoubtedly has an obligation to pay for the defense of those individuals who are too poor to finance their own defense, and ideally the defense counsel supplied to the indigent should be of the highest quality, for there are none who are in more desperate need of good counsel. Frankly, the quality of counsel generally supplied to the indigent leaves a great deal to be desired. It is the same old story: our society is more interested in supplying quality legal service to protect the accumulation of private wealth than in preserving the rights and the liberties of the poor. I undoubtedly would have ruled as Justice Warner did, and I was certainly not offended at the time by the ruling.

Eventually, however, I developed some reservations about the judge's decision in this particular case. On several occasions during the weeks that followed, Kunstler boasted to me that he did not charge legal fees for his courtroom services. He worked "for free," defending only those that he "loved," representing only causes that he "believed in." Late one afternoon as we stood on a subway platform waiting for a train, he explained to me that he earned a handsome income from speeches, television shows and other public appearances. His courtroom work, in effect, was voluntary. He did not need it to put bread on his table, and he took only those cases that appealed to him.

Apparently none of this posturing prevents Kunstler from taking money from the state for his legal services. Ironically, he is often as much a public employee as any police officer or correction guard. It is part of the paradox of the man that he will take money that he claims he does not need from the very government he hates and attacks at every possible opportunity.

Court-appointed attorneys serve at the pleasure of the court. They are not free to choose which cases will be assigned to them or to drop them without the court's consent. Indigent defendants are entitled to representation from competent counsel, but not to the counsel of their choice. If the rule were otherwise, it is easy to imagine every defendant in the country demanding William Kunstler, F. Lee Bailey, Percy Forman or some such superstar to defend him. Instead, cases are allotted in random fashion to those lawyers who choose to take court appointments. There is no hunting for "good" cases and no avoiding "bad" ones. It is purely the luck of the draw.

Kunstler does not operate this way. He enters the case of his choice as a "retained" counsel, and later wangles a court appointment. One wonders what would happen if a court ever asked Kunstler to supply legal representation to another defendant no less needy than James Richardson but perhaps less newsworthy.

Despite the above, I still feel the court was correct in

appointing Kunstler. I do have some doubts, however, about whether Kunstler should have asked for the appointment.

A pre-trial hearing is like a dress rehearsal. The trial judge presides; the defense and the prosecution examine and cross-examine witnesses. The defendant is present, and many of the witnesses who will be called at the trial itself appear and give testimony. The principal actors in the drama to follow have an opportunity to get to know one another and to practice their roles.

A pre-trial hearing is also a time of discovery. During the course of most such hearings, each side is forced to reveal much of its evidence, and the opposing lawyers have an opportunity to size up the witnesses that they will later try to discredit.

Just as there is no audience at a dress rehearsal, there is no jury at a pre-trial hearing. The first is performed in an empty theater, and the second is usually conducted in an empty courtroom. Both procedures are preparatory. But the ostensible purpose of the pre-trial hearing is not to afford both sides a dress rehearsal. In theory, it is held solely to protect the defendant from police abuses. Nevertheless, often the true importance of the pre-trial hearing lies in its rehearsal aspect rather than in its constitutional one. In many cases where the legal issues are not really in dispute, pre-trial hearings are still demanded by the defense and agreed to by the prosecution. Regardless of the judge's ruling on the legal issues, each side can always benefit from a dress rehearsal.

The *Richardson* pre-trial hearing began with law enforcement witnesses. Mike DuBoff, no longer a member of the district attorney's office, and practicing with a prosperous midtown law firm, gave testimony about the felony statement he had taken. Detectives Cruz and Gest testified, as did Patrolman Santiago. Each in turn related what Richardson had said in his presence on that night. Taken together, their testimony graphically depicted the confusion at Lincoln Hospital that evening. There had been too many law-enforcement people from too many agencies, all duplicating each other's efforts; there had been no coordinated effort to conduct a single investigation. The testimony made this clear. It was also clear that James Richardson had in fact been talking his head off that night. There was no doubt that he had made the seven statements attributed to him and would have made seven more if asked. On that night at least, Richardson had been eager to tell his side of the story.

The testimony also revealed—and Kunstler did not really challenge it—that Richardson had been advised of his rights many times. Each of the police officers stated that he had reminded the defendant of them at the outset. They had done so automatically, "the rights" being a catechism that had been drummed into them from the moment they had become policemen. Whether or not Richardson had understood them, there could be no doubt that he had heard them.

Ironically, Kunstler made some headway with former Assistant District Attorney DuBoff, the one lawyer and the last individual who questioned the prisoner that night. By the time DuBoff reached him, Richardson had been in some sort of contact with an attorney.

MR. KUNSTLER: Now, Mr. Richardson told you after you first mentioned "lawyer" to him that he had a lawyer coming, didn't he?

A. That's correct.

Q. Did you stop then and wait for that lawyer to get there?

A. No, I did not.

Q. You went ahead, did you not?

A. That's correct.

Q. And in fact he reminded you twice that he had an attorney coming?

A. Yes.

Q. Did you ask him the name of his attorney?

A. No, I didn't.

Q. Did you tell him you would wait until his attorney got there before you continued the questioning?

A. I told—I asked him if he still wished to tell me what happened.

In effect, Kunstler had succeeded in establishing that DuBoff had been wrong in failing to terminate his questioning after Richardson told him that he had been in touch with an attorney, and was well on his way toward having the Court suppress the stenographic statement that DuBoff had taken that night. But he did not fare nearly so well with the police witnesses, for there was no legal flaw to the statements they had taken. Instead, he was reduced to conducting a lengthy and essentially trivial cross-examination on the ability of the various officers to take longhand notes. This tactic got him nowhere.

My role during the pre-trial hearings was basically a passive one. I merely put my witnesses on the stand, let them tell their stories, and sat back while Kunstler tried to discredit them. My witnesses were well prepared, I believed that their testimony was truthful, and I was anxious to see how they would stand up to Kunstler's famous skill at cross-examination. They did well; I could afford to sit back.

The heart of this pre-trial hearing proved to be medical rather than legal, for the issue truly in dispute was Richardson's physical condition at the time he was being questioned. Kunstler contended that his client had been in such agony that rational communication with him was impossible. He also took the position that the medical treatment the defendant received had so sedated or drugged him that he could not have been lucid and coherent.

I had anticipated this argument, and during the course of my preparations had made careful inquiries. Without exception, the individuals who had seen him that night insisted that Richardson had been in complete control of his faculties throughout the evening. Everyone agreed that he had spoken in normal conversational tones and had given responsive answers to every question asked him. No one could recall his crying out in pain, groaning, fainting or in any other way signifying great distress. However, on one or two occasions he had complained quietly of discomfort in his shoulder.

To clinch my case, I called as a witness at the pre-trial hearing Dr. Roger Smoke, the surgeon who had treated Richardson that night. He testified in part as follows:

MR. PHILLIPS: Now, Doctor, when you saw Mr. Richardson, would you describe for us his appearance . . . ?

A. At the time I saw him he was quite composed. He was lying on the stretcher. I went and asked him a little bit of his past history, what had happened to him, and recorded my findings on the chart.

Q. At that time was he able to lucidly and intelligently respond to the questions that you put to him?

A. Yes.

Q. Was there anything there at all irrational about his behavior?

A. Nothing that I remember.

Q. Did he have any difficulty speaking?

A. Not that I recall.

Q. Do you recall the tone and quality of his voice as you spoke to him?

A. As I recall, he was very polite, very reasonable in any requests made, very receptive to any questions or any advice that I had to offer.

I also asked Dr. Smoke whether Richardson's catheterization or the intravenous fluids he had received had appeared to affect his ludidity or rationality. He replied that they did not. I asked him about the effect of the Demerol and Nembutal injections he had prescribed, and he answered that throughout the night Richardson had remained alert and responsive, and that both drugs given to Richardson that night had been in such amounts that it was highly unlikely they would have affected his rationality. Dr. Smoke's testimony had effectively laid to rest Kunstler's medical claim.

As it turned out, Kunstler also had a physician he wished to call as a witness. He announced to the court that the man would arrive at about noon and that he had never met him. This casual remark told me a great deal. Kunstler had not even interviewed his own witness! I had spent months interviewing my witnesses and mastering all the complexities of my case, and here was Kunstler casually admitting that he had not bothered to meet with an important witness!

In any event, a Dr. Richard Taft gave testimony on behalf of James Richardson. He had not treated the prisoner that night, and in fact had only seen Richardson for a few seconds when he had first been brought into the emergency room. Dr. Taft stated that at that time Richardson was bleeding heavily from the head. I imagine that the purpose of this testimony was to suggest that Richardson had been beaten by the police as well as shot. I was distressed by this testimony. To be charitable—though at the time I did not feel charitable—I believe that Dr. Taft's testimony was simply mistaken. I had photographs that had been taken of Richardson on that night and they revealed no head injuries, not even the slightest scratch. His hospital records did not mention any head injuries and none of my witnesses, including Dr. Smoke, had seen any.

Dr. Taft also testified about the effect of Demerol and Nembutal on a patient such as Richardson. Predictably, he differed completely with his colleague and the half-dozen other physicians I had also questioned on the subject. In his opinion, these drugs would have clouded James Richardson's mind and effectively rendered him irrational.

With Dr. Taft's testimony, Kunstler rested. He did not choose to put Richardson on the stand.

Pat Skagen sat in the same seat in the second row of the audience section of the courtroom throughout the hearing and the trial. She never left the seat for a moment and never said a word. Each morning, when the hearing began, she was there, and she never left before the end of the day. For her, this was no dress rehearsal.

Kunstler hit full stride when he made his arguments at the end of the hearing. But though he went on for a good half-hour, his argument can be stated briefly. In his view, on the night of June 28, 1972, James Richardson was "a wounded man in shock, going through enormous discomfort . . ." Such a man, he contended, could not intelligently waive his right to remain silent. Closing with a rhetorical flourish, he told the court that the failure to suppress Richardson's statements in this case would be tantamount to scrapping the Fifth Amendment of the United States Constitution. It was a masterly bit of advocacy.

I did my best to pour cold water on Kunstler's rhetoric, pointing out to the court that Richardson's statements to his civilian friends (Miss Johnson and Blondell Gimbell) had not been made to law enforcement officials or at their request. They had been freely and spontaneously given, and as such did not fall within the scope of the *Miranda* decision;* they would be admissible in evidence regardless of Richardson's physical condition or whether or not he had been properly advised of his rights. The Fifth Amendment does not protect individuals from confessions made to other civilians. I argued that even if the court were to find merit in Kunstler's arguments about the other statements, they could not apply to these two.

I also took sharp issue with Kunstler on the question of Richardson's physical condition. Without exception, all the testimony from witnesses who had actually spoken to Richardson that night established that he had been lucid and rational throughout. The very transcript of his final statement to Assist-

---

Miranda v. *Arizona* is the landmark Supreme Court case (1966) which established the principle that a confession to a police officer could not be used in court unless the suspect being questioned was first advised of his rights.

ant District Attorney DuBoff was eloquent proof of this; indeed, what better proof could there be of the fact that he had understood his rights than the simple fact that, as the rights advised, he had contacted an attorney? I dismissed Kunstler's assertions about his client's being in shock as nothing more than wishful thinking.

I had legal precedent to cite to Justice Warner and had prepared a memorandum of law on the subject. I was able to cite other cases, with defendants far more serously injured than Richardson had been, in which other courts had refused to suppress confessions obtained in hospital wards. I did not want the court to suppress those statements.

Justice Warner listened silently and attentively to our arguments, then without further ado recessed the case and retired to his chambers to prepare his decision. The wait was the first tense period of the trial for me. A great deal was at stake, and I did not relish the prospect of trying the case without the statements.

At the next session of the court, Justice Warner announced his decision. After a lengthy recapitulation of the evidence adduced by both sides he offered his findings:

JUSTICE WARNER: This Court finds that the defendant made seven statements, alleged[ly] inculpating himself and at the same time some exculpating himself.

At 6 P.M. on June 28th, 1972, in the emergency room at Lincoln Hospital, the defendant gave a statement to Miss Johnson which . . . was overheard by Patrolman Santiago.

At 6:45 P.M., also in the emergency room, the defendant gave a statement to Detective Cruz, New York City Police Department.

At 7:15 P.M. in Ward 4B, the defendant gave a statement to Patrolman Santiago.

At 7:30 P.M. in Ward 4B, Patrolman Santiago overheard a conversation between the defendant and the cousin, Blondell Gimbell.

At approximately 8:15 P.M. in Ward 4B, Detective Richard Gest received a statement . . . and at about 8:30 P.M. in Ward 4B, Detective Louis Cruz received a second statement . . . At 10 P.M. in Ward 4B, Assistant District Attorney Duboff received a statement . . . which . . . was simultaneously recorded by a stenographer.

The proof establishes that this defendant was not in such pain or that the pain he suffered did not prevent his understanding questions propounded to him, and that he fully understood what he was asked and realized the statements that he made.

In this regard, the Court notes that Webster's Collegiate Dictionary defines pain as localized physical suffering. . . . the Court further notes that the defendant complained of pain . . . in his shoulder, that the defendant was conscious at all times and coherent in his speech, cooperative in his conduct, and rational in his intellect.

The Court further finds there was no coercion, either physical or mental, exerted upon the defendant that caused him to make the alleged inculpatory and exculpatory statements.

That the defendant sent for Detective Cruz in order to give him the 8:30 statement, that the medication administered to the defendant did not affect questioning and making coherent answers to his questioners.

That the fact that the defendant was additionally suffering from severe gunshot wounds . . . does not, per se, compel the finding that the admissions were produced by mental coercion or that he was thus rendered easy prey for mental compulsion.

That the statements given to Assistant District Attorney DuBoff shall be inadmissible as evidence . . . because Mr. DuBoff continued to question the defendant and take his statement after having been informed by the defendant that he had a lawyer coming . . .

The Court further finds that under the Miranda principle, the Assistant District Attorney should have ended his interview at that point, pending the arrival of the defendant's attorney, or at least inquired further of the defendant regarding the attorney. That the two statements made by the defendant to Detective

Cruz were voluntarily made, and [that] prior to both statements, Detective Cruz advised the defendant of his constitutional rights as required by Miranda, and that the defendant indicated that he understood them and . . . intelligently and voluntarily waived these rights.

That the statement made to Detective Gest was voluntarily made and . . . [that] Detective Gest advised the defendant of his constitutional rights . . . and that the defendant indicated that he understood them, and . . . intelligently and voluntarily waived his rights.

The Court further finds that the alleged conversation between the defendant and his cousin, and also another conversation with Miss Johnson which was overheard by Patrolman Santiago, are admissible against the defendant and not subject to the Miranda guidelines, in that the statement was not made in response to any questions posed by a law-enforcement officer . . .

This court therefore concludes that all of the statements and/or confessions heretofore mentioned, except the statement . . . given to Assistant District Attorney DuBoff were voluntary and the result of an intelligent and knowing waiver . . . of his constitutional rights . . .

As to the defendant's condition, the evidence clearly reveals that [he] was not prevented from resisting interrogation if he so desired, that he was rational, lucid and coherent . . . and had full knowledge of all of the pertinent circumstances during the questioning.

Accordingly, the motion to suppress the admissions or confessions as involuntary and inadmissible are denied except the statement to Assistant D.A. DuBoff . . . As to that statement, the motion is granted.

22

Voir Dire

The following morning at nine-thirty a hundred prospective jurors trooped into the courtroom, buzzed with conversation, took their seats and folded their newspapers. They seemed mildly curious about the experience to come. About a third of them had served as jurors before.

Facing the front of the courtroom, I resisted the urge to turn around and size up the panel. There would be ample opportunity to do so later on; right now, the curtain was going up and appearances were all-important.

When Justice Warner entered the courtroom, Morris Krohn, the clerk of the court cried out, "All rise! Hear ye! Hear ye! All those having business before this the Supreme Court of the State of New York in and for the County of Bronx, give your attention and draw near. Presiding, the Honorable Ivan Warner, Justice of the Supreme Court."

We all rose and remained standing until Justice Warner had taken his seat. Then, with a nod from him, we all sat down, much like a religious congregation at the close of a prayer.

After a pause Justice Warner broke the silence. He introduced himself to the panel and told them that they were in a criminal trial term of the Supreme Court, Bronx County. He introduced James Richardson and advised the panel that the defendant had been indicted by the grand jury of Bronx County and charged with seven crimes. Without further ado, his voice clear and forceful, he began to read the indictment: "Supreme Court in and for the County of Bronx. The People of the State of New York against James Richardson, defendant. The Grand Jury of the County of Bronx, by this indictment accuse the defendant of the crime of murder . . ."

With this the panel of prospective jurors became hushed. They now realized that they had been summoned on serious business, and had the first inkling of the role they would be asked to play.

The judge read on: "The said defendant . . . while engaged in the commission of a felony, to wit, escape in the second degree . . . caused the death of one John Skagen, a police officer of the New York City Transit Authority Police Department."

There was a collective gasp, and though the judge continued to read, I do not believe that the jurors continued to listen. The possibility of being a juror in a cop-killing case took time to sink in. The atmosphere in the courtroom was grim by the time Justice Warner finished reading the indictment.

Then I was introduced to the panel. I stood, turned around and looked at my audience. One hundred individuals looked back at me. Overall, they were somewhat more white than black, more male than female, and more middle-aged than young. It appeared to be a typical panel of prospective jurors for Bronx County. After a few seconds I sat down.

Now the judge introduced Kunstler. He, too, stood, turned and faced his audience. Again there was a gasp; fully half the panel realized that they were looking at a celebrity. The rest of the jurors buzzed with questions and quickly learned from their neighbors who William Kunstler was.

With Kunstler's introduction, the prologue was completed and the voir dire commenced.

A voir dire is the process by which twelve individuals are selected to sit as a jury in a criminal case. The object of the voir dire, at least in theory, is to find twelve people who will be fair, impartial arbiters of fact. Realistically, nobody expects to find in such a panel twelve angels descended from heaven. The hope is that a dozen individuals can be found who will be reasonably even-handed in the case to be tried.

Although impartiality is the theoretical goal sought by the voir dire, it certainly was not what either Kunstler or I was looking for. Frankly, each of us was hoping for a jury that would be predisposed to favor our side. Kunstler would gladly have accepted a jury of twelve members of the Black Liberation Army, and I would have been equally content with twelve Irish Catholic policemen. Neither of us was being honest when we repeatedly told the prospective jurors that we were only seeking people who could give both sides a fair shake. To be charitable, it might be fair to say that for the opposing attorneys the voir dire is a performance in which they are required to ignore the literal truth for a time and assume foreordained roles. If we ended up with an impartial jury in this case—and I believe that we did—it was not because either Kunstler or I desired one. It happened because each of us was more or less successful in thwarting the other's intentions.

The mechanics of the voir dire are set forth by statute. Twelve prospective jurors are called into the jury box and are questioned first by the court, then by the assistant district attorney and the defense attorney, respectively. Any potential juror who displays either a bias or an unwillingness or inability to serve may be excused by consent if both counsel and the court agree. Often as many as half the panel are excused because they claim to have some pressing personal or business reason that will conflict with their service. By and large, such excuses are accepted uncritically by all concerned. Neither Kunstler nor I had any desire to keep an unwilling juror imprisoned in the jury box for many weeks. Such a person would seethe with hostility, and his ultimate actions would be unpredictable.

Other prospective jurors could be "challenged for cause" by either attorney, meaning that the individual had expressed an opinion which, as a matter of law, disqualified him from sitting in that particular case. Such challenges are addressed by the attorneys to the court, and after legal argument the judge decides whether or not to accept the challenge.

After the challenges for cause are exercised and those who have been excused by consent are gone, each side is permitted to exercise "peremptory challenges." Such challenges are exercised at the sole discretion of either attorney, no legal justification being required for their use. In a murder case, each side is permitted up to twenty peremptory challenges.

The exercising of peremptory challenges becomes something of a game. Each side attempts to hoard them and hopes to have some left over after his opponent has exhausted his allotment. By judiciously using his remaining peremptory challenges, an attorney in such a position can determine who the remaining jurors will be—an enormous advantage.

Inevitably, there is a great deal of gambling, guesswork, gamesmanship and bluffing that goes into the exercise of peremptory challenges. Much amateur applied psychology is used, and recently such exotic arts as body reading have been brought into play. All of this is based upon the questionable assumption that it is possible, after relatively brief contact, to determine what a stranger's biases really are. Regardless, the process of selecting a jury is an interesting and revealing experience.

Though the attorneys are seeking to uncover the prejudices of the prospective jurors in a voir dire, as often as not what is ultimately revealed are the prejudices of the lawyers themselves. In using his peremptory challenges an attorney gives a sure clue to his own attitudes. Feelings about race are perhaps the best example of this phenomenon. Traditionally, prosecutors have attempted to keep blacks off juries on the theory that they will be predisposed to acquit. Conversely, defense attorneys have tended over the years to seek out black jurors.

I have never accepted the racial view held by many prosecutors. In my experience, black jurors are generally more oriented toward law-and-order and the prosecution than many of the more affluent and sheltered white jurors. The victims of most street crimes are black, and there is no group of citizens in Bronx County more in need of and more grateful for police protection—when they receive it—than the great majority of law-abiding black citizens. Though it is hard to generalize, I have also found black jurors to be more street-wise than most whites, and thus better able to realistically evaluate evidence of street crimes. I have never detected any evidence of unwillingness to convict on the part of black jurors and have always welcomed them on my juries.

Kunstler also wanted black jurors—any black juror at all. In fact, though we eventually went through two hundred individuals to arrive at a twelve-person jury, and though Kunstler ultimately employed all twenty of his peremptory challenges, not once did he challenge a potential black juror. On the other hand, he did challenge every Irish and Italian prospect who was not excused for cause or by consent. He also excluded every white male who appeared to be over forty-five. It soon became clear that he wanted as many blacks as possible, and failing that, young Jews or Puerto Ricans.

Philosophy aside, from a purely pragmatic point of view Kunstler's jury-selection strategy was badly out of touch with the realities of New York. Perhaps in the South it is possible to make sharp racial distinctions in jury selection, but it just doesn't work in Bronx County. Whatever its origins, the strategy of the defense was simplistic, and played right into my hands.

Once I realized what Kunstler was up to, I was quickly able to stack the jury with a large number of conservative, law-and-order black jurors. For instance, one of the men the defense accepted was a middle-aged black man who had once served as a federal law enforcement officer; he had two nephews, with whom he said he was close, both of whom were transit cops! How Kunstler could possibly permit an individual with such ties to law enforcement to sit on a cop-killing case was beyond my comprehension. I was delighted to see this man sworn in.

Eventually, after ten jurors had been selected, Kunstler ran out of peremptory challenges. I had used fourteen and had six left. After he used his last challenge, Kunstler asked to approach the bench to make a legal application outside the hearing of the jury. Suddenly, after two weeks of jury selection, he announced that he was challenging the entire panel as being too old and hopelessly biased against his client. He asked the court either to declare a mistrial or to grant him additional peremptory challenges.

Naturally, I opposed Kunstler's application. By then there were ten sworn jurors, seven of whom appeared to be in their twenties or thirties, and the defense had achieved its obvious goal of selecting a substantial number of young jurors. In addition, I objected to Kunstler's making this application after almost two weeks of voir dire. He had known the makeup of the panel for two weeks and had made no complaint, but now, when he had run out of challenges and things seemed to be going my way, he was seeking to change the rules of the game. It was as if a baseball team that was behind in the last of the ninth suddenly demanded that the game be extended for three more innings. I argued that Kunstler should have made his application at the beginning of the voir dire, not at its conclusion.

Justice Warner refused to grant Kunstler's application, and we returned to our seats. Among the next prospective jurors to be called was a young black man who worked for the New York City Department of Social Services. In the course of questioning him I sensed that he was hostile, and since he also stated that he was a long-time admirer of Kunstler I accordingly exercised a peremptory challenge. Instantly Kunstler leaped from his seat, his face contorted with rage, and yelled to the jury, "See what a racist prosecution we are dealing with! He challenges every damn black and young person!" In a second I was on my feet also yelling at the top of my lungs, trying to drown out Kunstler's outburst. Reacting promptly, Justice Warner ordered Kunstler and myself into his robing room immediately. As soon as we entered it Kunstler's features broke into a smile. I was livid. Five of the ten jurors selected at that point were black, and seven of the ten would be characterized as young rather than old. Kunstler had challenged every Irish and Italian juror, regardless of age or sex, as well as every white juror who appeared to be old, regardless of sex, religion or ethnic identification, and yet he was accusing me of being racist!

Kunstler's contention was ridiculous on its very face, as anyone looking at the ten sworn jurors—and, I hoped, they themselves—could see. Nevertheless, his outburst worried me greatly. Attorneys are sometimes persuasive not because they are truthful but because they are impassioned and plausible. I felt that one or more of the jurors might ignore the evidence to come and be taken in by Kunstler's posturing, and I heatedly expressed this concern to Justice Warner while Kunstler stood there smiling.

In the end, the judge simply warned Kunstler that he would not tolerate any such outburst in the future. We then went back into the courtroom, and the judge solemnly admonished the jury to disregard what Kunstler had said. I took little comfort from this; there was simply no way for the jurors to erase from their minds what Kunstler had shouted, and, of course, he was well aware of this.

There is much more to a voir dire than the simple process of questioning and selecting jurors. In addition to the gamesmanship and psychology, a voir dire is an opportunity for the attorneys to educate their juries about the theories of their cases. It is also an opportunity to plant seeds of doubt that they hope will produce a favorable verdict. It is a chance to predispose jurors to be receptive to the attorney's cause.

This "education" is accomplished under the guise of questioning jurors about their possible prejudices. An attorney will ask essentially rhetorical questions of jurors, the purpose of which is not so much to elicit an answer as to make those listening think about and accept the attorney's view of a particular problem. For instance, I would ask a juror whether he felt he could convict Richardson of the gun-possession charge even though I could not physically produce the weapon in court. After explaining that the law did not require the actual gun itself to prove my case, I would ask the juror if he had ever thrown a rock into the ocean or a lake. The person would answer yes, and then I would ask whether the fact that this rock could not be recovered would create any doubt that in fact it had been thrown. Of course the answer would be no, and then I would explain that the same principle applied to the gun charge. If the evidence presented at the trial persuaded the juror that Richardson had possessed the gun, its absence from the courtroom did not mean that the defendant was innocent. The purpose of these questions was not to discover the juror's prejudices, but to make a point that might help the jury to convict. It was an opportunity to neutralize a possible weakness in my case—even to turn it into an advantage. I was laying a foundation for arguments I would be making later.

Kunstler also had some educating to do. With almost every prospective juror he stressed one theme. "Can you accept the possibility that the government, the police and the district attorney's office could try to frame an innocent black man for a crime they themselves committed?" "Can you accept the possibility that a police officer could come into this court, swear an oath before God to tell the truth, and then lie to you?"

"Can you accept the possibility that a conspiracy exists to send James Richardson to jail?" With these and other questions, he was preparing the jury for his own theory of the case.

During my part of the voir dire, I took great pains to agree with Kunstler's questions, but not with his philosophy. I would say to a juror, "Of course it is possible for a police officer to lie, and of course it is possible for the government to conspire to frame an innocent man—you understand that, don't you? I agree with Mr. Kunstler when he says that these things are possible. But the real question here is not whether these things are possible, but whether they actually occurred or will occur in this particular case; do you understand that?" I wanted the panel to see that I was not afraid of the defense's thesis and was ready to confront it head-on.

My strategy throughout the trial was to be as low-key and reasonable as possible, and to win the jury over with quiet common sense rather than self-righteous piety. It seemed to me that the best way to cope with Kunstler's flamboyance and apocalyptic rhetoric was not to answer in kind. If I came on strong and battled Kunstler every inch of the way, I would only give credence to his thesis that he was fighting a vicious, vindictive opponent. Instead, I tailored my conduct to contrast, and sought at all times to appear decent and fair.

During the voir dire, Kunstler and I revealed a great deal about our hopes and expectations. I was afraid of the possibility of a hung jury; as a result, I asked many rhetorical questions designed to impress upon the panel the importance of collective deliberation and of reaching a unanimous verdict. I asked each juror whether he would close his ears to the opinions and arguments of his fellow jurors, or whether he would listen carefully and respectfully to what the other person had to say. I wanted those jurors to really deliberate and to reach a verdict. Kunstler, on the other hand, understood that a hung jury would not be harmful to his client. Richardson could remain at liberty for months, even years, before a re-trial, and the passage of additional time could only help him. Consequently, during his questioning, Kunstler impressed upon each juror the importance of his individual conscience and asked whether the individual would ever vote to convict a man he believed to be innocent just because the other jurors urged him to it.

Day after day the voir dire went on as Kunstler and I took turns preaching our gospels. We were on our feet for hours at a time. It was an exhausting and ultimately a tedious business. The judge and those jurors already selected had to suffer through every moment of it, and we were all relieved when it was over.

During the voir dire I began to acquire a limited insight into Kunstler's character. I came to realize that he was vulnerable to attacks on his self-esteem. From time to time I tried to irritate him and shake his composure.

At that time Kunstler was more than twice as old as I, and one did not have to be perceptive to realize that he was sensitive about his age. I could not resist the temptation to exploit this weakness. Over and over, I stressed to the panel the fact that Kunstler was an old-timer, while I was a youngster. He was a "world-famous lawyer" with a well-deserved reputation for eloquence, whereas I was just a kid who didn't even belong in the same courtroom with this great man. I warned the panel that Kunstler was a better lawyer than I and that they would be more impressed with him than with me. But then I added that, of course, it was not the skills of the lawyers that counted, but the facts of the case and what the jurors believed. I asked prospective jurors whether they would vote to acquit merely because the old-timer could easily get the better of me, and, of course, they answered no.

The point of such questions was not only to get under Kunstler's skin but to cast myself as an underdog in the minds of the jury. All the world loves a David, and I wanted the jury to think of me as such. Everybody loves to see a Goliath get his just deserts, and I wanted the jury to think of Kunstler in those terms.

Since it was one of his own favorite postures, Kunstler was not insensitive to the virtues of the underdog's role, and he was irritated by my characterization. He assured the jury that he was not that old and that I was not that young. He took great pains to praise my skills as an attorney, and tried to dispel the idea that I was an underdog.

After eight full days we succeeded in selecting twelve jurors and four alternates. All told, the jury consisted of seven men and five women. There were five whites, five blacks and two Hispanic jurors. Most of them were well under forty years of age.

At twenty minutes before noon on October 7, 1974, we were ready to begin taking testimony. Justice Warner then dismissed the jury, instructing them to return at two o'clock, and for the first of what would come to seem like a thousand times, he admonished them to keep an open mind, not to discuss the case with anyone and not to form any opinion about the guilt or innocence of James Richardson.

23

Opening Shots

After the jurors were dismissed I spoke up. Before I delivered my opening statement, I wished to clear up some legal issues which I knew would arise. I planned to inform the jury that on June 28, 1972, James Richardson was a wanted man, and to introduce into evidence the two warrants outstanding against him. I spoke up in advance because I anticipated that Kunstler would object vigorously to my mentioning these warrants, and so I wanted the court to give an advance ruling on their admissibility. I was not obliged to seek an advance ruling, for I believed that I was legally entitled to discuss the warrants, and I could very well have mentioned their existence during my opening statement in good faith. Such an approach would have presented defense and the court with a *fait accompli*. Kunstler could then argue law to his heart's content, but never succeed in undoing what I had said. This would be quite an advantage.

Nevertheless, I decided to raise the issue in advance and risk the possibility (not a great one, I thought) that the court would rule against me. I did this because I realized that if I mentioned the warrants without warning, it would only provoke Kunstler. I was concerned that it might lead to an outburst, perhaps even to violent legal arguments in front of the jury, and I did not want this to happen. I wanted to argue law leisurely and quietly in the absence of the jury. This was preferable to the possibility of creating an impression in Kunstler's mind—or worse, in the jury's—that I was trying to pull a fast one. More important, I was eager to establish in this trial a pattern of anticipating and resolving legal issues peacefully. Above all, I wanted to give Kunstler few possibilities for carrying on in front of the jury.

Arguing law with Justice Warner, I contended that the warrants were admissible against Richardson because they provided proof of his motive for trying to escape John Skagen's arrest. I reasoned that a wanted man, knowing that he faced the likelihood of incarceration in two counties, would have a powerful incentive to flee, and I felt that the jury had a right to hear about the warrants. I had done my homework and was well prepared. My research had located a number of cases that supported my contentions, and I cited them to the judge. As always, he listened impassively, but he took notes.

Kunstler had known about the existence of the warrants, for I had brought them to his attention weeks earlier. He must have known—or should have known—that I would seek to introduce them, for they were hardly trivial pieces of evidence. They could hurt Richardson badly because they would characterize him as a wanted criminal, as a man who had sought to escape justice twice before. It was important that the defense fight the admission of the warrants. Kunstler asked for an opportunity to do legal research on this question during the lunch break, and Judge Warner permitted the recess.

After lunch Kunstler argued convincingly that the prejudice to Richardson of parading his criminal past before the jury far outweighed the probative value that this evidence contained about his state of mind on June 28, 1972. During the recess, he had located the cases I had cited in the Bar Association library, and now he argued that these cases were inapplicable.

Justice Warner listened, and then turned to me and asked whether it was my contention that John Skagen had known that Richardson was a wanted man. I replied that this seemed highly unlikely; my point was that Richardson, not Skagen, had been aware of the existence of the warrants, and it was Richardson's, not Skagen's, state of mind on which I was trying to shed light. The court then asked me whether I was claiming that the warrants were the only reason why Richardson had taken flight that afternoon. This was not my position, for I knew that ultimately I would argue to the jury that the prospect of a felony gun charge had been the primary motivation behind Richardson's escape, and I said as much.

Justice Warner ruled against me; he excluded all reference to the warrants from the trial. This upset me, and I was angry at myself for seeking an advance ruling. In retrospect, however, I have come to believe that I followed the correct course, for I am no longer certain that my legal position was correct. Had I plunged ahead and mentioned the warrants, I might have committed an error that could have led to reversal on appeal. Equally important was the calm and amicable tone that the trial took on as a result of this way of proceeding. In the long run this was far more valuable than whatever tactical advantage I might have gained by mentioning the warrants. In any event, the jury never did learn that Richardson was a wanted man.

The jury was ushered into the courtroom and took their seats amid a hush. As Morris Krohn, the court clerk, read out their names, each of them responded. Then Judge Warner read them his brief preliminary instructions, outlining for them the various stages of a trial and informing them about some of the rudiments of trial procedure. They would be the sole judges of the facts of the case, while he would be the sole judge of the law. Then the judge turned to me and instructed me to proceed with my opening statement. The stage was all mine.

I had considered two possible approaches in my opening statement. On the one hand, I could have deliberately kept my opening remarks short and vague. By speaking in the broadest generalities about what I intended to prove, I would let my proof speak for itself, and allow the particulars of my case to emerge during the course of the trial. Such a tactic would promise little to the jury, but would leave me with maximum flexibility. I would be able to wait and see how my witnesses stood up under cross-examination and what kind of defense Kunstler would put up. Then, in summation, at the end, I would be able to frame my arguments without being embarrassed by anything I had said at the beginning. Having made few claims of proof, no one would be able to accuse me later of failing to deliver. I had seen many cases lost by attorneys who had started out by promising too much. They had presented cases that were more than adequate, that should have resulted in success, but were lost not because they were weak but because they failed to live up to the extravagant claims made for them in advance. It is dangerous to inflate a jury's expectations. There was much to be said for a short opening.

The other alternative was a more detailed opening statement. I knew that this approach was more risky—but also perhaps more rewarding. A forceful opening that dotted the i's and crossed the t's offered an opportunity to condition the jury to accept the evidence that I would ultimately offer. It would provide them with an authoritative overview of my case by painting a picture for them of what had really happened Later, as each witness gave testimony, they would be able to place it in context in the overall picture. I could make promises, and if these were kept during the course of the trial, my credibility would be powerfully enhanced by the time of summation. At least as important, a detailed opening statement would give me the opportunity to impose, right at the outset, my own style and theories on the trial. By being aggressive, I could stress my strengths and minimize my weaknesses.

Given the nature of my case, I felt I had no choice; I had to risk a detailed, comprehensive opening statement. My case was just too complicated; I had too many witnesses, too many exhibits and too many documents for the jury to digest easily without some orientation. I was dependent upon a great deal of expert testimony, and I had to alert the jury to its importance. I had to impress upon them that a combination of ballistics and medical evidence was the key to understanding what had really happened.

It was also imperative that I steal Kunstler's thunder. I had to be the one to inform the jury that John Skagen had been shot not only by James Richardson but also by George Wieber. I could not permit this to become a damaging revelation; I did not want it to appear that I was hiding it from the jury. I was being candid with the jury in my opening, and I hoped that they would realize this and would like me for it. In addition, by weaving this painful fact into the overall tapestry, I hoped to cast it in a perspective that would actually strengthen rather than weaken my case. By telling them about it in my own words, I would be laying a foundation: in effect, I would be asking the jury to look upon Wieber as a victim, not as a perpetrator.

My opening statement lasted well over an hour. I was low-key in my delivery and stayed away from theatrics. I kept it simple and held the jury's attention, maintaining eye contact with several of them. The courtroom was silent and I could sense that they understood me. I was getting my message across: James Richardson had murdered John Skagen.

Kunstler chose not to give an opening statement. As defense counsel, this was his privilege. When he rose to announce this, I could see surprise and disappointment on the faces of the jurors. They wanted to hear Richardson's side of the story and Kunstler's famous eloquence.

All in all, I was pleased with the opening. I felt that a positive tone had been set; I had seized the initiative and defined the case. I had made my promise; now I had to deliver.

24

The People's Case

Justice Warner proved to be a hard taskmaster who drove the trial forward relentlessly. Court opened at 9:30 A.M. sharp, and no excuses for delay were accepted. We recessed for lunch at 1 P.M., reconvened at 2 P.M. and adjourned for the day no earlier than five o'clock. The pace was nonstop. We were generally permitted one five-to-ten-minute recess each morning and afternoon, the judge's only concession to fatigue and the call of nature.

The court personnel were not happy. Accustomed to the easygoing pace common in many other trial parts, they did not take kindly to Justice Warner's energetic ways. His part was not a popular assignment for the court officers. Without any prisoner to guard, there was little for them to do. They grumbled—though never when the judge was within earshot.

Unlike the court officers, the stenographers had good cause for discontent, for the hard-driving pace subjected them to considerable strain. Physically, the demands on them were immense. It is no mean feat to take down every word uttered in a fast-moving and emotional trial. Some of the witnesses mumbled or whispered incoherently, others were nervous and spoke very rapidly, while still others rambled on and on in a dead monotone. The doctors and pathologists who appeared peppered their testimony with medical jargon. Somehow the stenographers had to get all this down, and also catch everything that Kunstler and I said. From time to time we would interrupt, make objections, argue with each other, rant and rave, and generally disrupt the orderly flow of testimony. All of this had to be recorded accurately. Then, when the day was over and everyone else had departed, the stenographers had to type up the trial transcript. In a murder case, "daily copy" is required, and each morning the judge and the lawyers have to be given a transcript of the previous day's testimony.

I also would have been happy to go more slowly; I found the forced pace difficult to sustain. There was little or no time to reflect upon what had happened, or to collect one's thoughts and plan for what lay ahead. But Justice Warner would tolerate no delays, and there were none.

Heretofore, when trying a case, it had been my practice to call one witness to the stand and to leave the others downstairs in my office waiting to testify. Then as each person finished I would request a five-minute recess while my next witness was brought upstairs. These pauses were invaluable; they permitted a short breather during which I could relax and prepare myself mentally for the new testimony. In addition, such recesses offered the opportunity to have a word or two with the new witness before he took the stand. Often it is important to calm people down and offer a few last words of encouragement or advice. I had counted upon having these short recesses. But Justice Warner would have none of this. At the outset of the trial he instructed me that as each witness took the stand, the following one was to wait in the hall outside the courtroom. When one was done, the next was to take his place immediately.

During the Richardson trial I was working a fourteen-hour day. By seven-thirty each morning I was in my office to prepare for the coming day's testimony. Dom Cuccio, Bob Maguire and some of the other detectives would meet me there then, and we would go over what had to be done while I was in court. There were always witnesses to be transported to and from court, evidence to be obtained from the various clerks' offices, and last-minute minor crises to be dealt with. I would never have made it without the assistance of these detectives.

After this council of war, I would try to speak briefly to all the witnesses due to testify that morning, for I could not do so once court was in session. I felt that at the very least I owed these people, some of whom I had not seen in months, a little encouragement. Also, especially as the trial wore on, I found that new and unanticipated questions arose.

The forty other murder cases sitting in my files could not be ignored, either, and each morning it seemed that one or another of them urgently demanded my attention. A defendant who had been stubbornly holding out for a trial would decide to reconsider an earlier plea offer; his lawyer would call to iron out the details; and I would have to take time out to negotiate. Another defendant would serve us with a writ of habeas corpus which had to be answered. In a third case a key witness would be threatened and would demand protection. Day after day there were endless details to be handled before court opened. But at nine-thirty sharp, come what may, I had to be in court; no excuses were accepted. From then until five o'clock, with an hour off for lunch, we worked.

Physically and mentally there are few activities more exhausting than the trial of a criminal case. In court not only is one constantly on stage and maintaining appearances, but part of one's mind is busy keeping track of the many questions each witness must be asked. I had to keep these in my head, for I did not want the jury to see me referring to notes. Such paper might be construed by a cynical juror as a prepared and concocted script, and I did not want to create a false impression.

But it is not only the questions that require concentration; the answers are just as important. It is surprisingly difficult to listen to a witness's answers when you know what he is going to say. Nevertheless, it was essential to listen critically, for the same answers that were familiar to me were quite new to everyone else. I had to try to hear the testimony as if for the first time; it was the only way to gauge its impact.

Throughout the trial I kept an eye on the jury. I wanted to be sure that they were attentive. I needed their approval, and stayed on the alert for nodding heads, quizzical looks or any other clue that might give me an idea of what they were thinking.

I also had to watch Kunstler carefully. After his first outburst during the voir dire, I was waiting for a repetition, and tried to be poised to respond immediately, especially while he was cross-examining my witnesses. I felt that at any moment he was capable of letting slip some prejudicial or improper remark designed to appeal to the racial or political sympathies of the jury, and I was determined to forestall this. As it turned out, Kunstler was relatively restrained thereafter. I could not foresee this, however, and whenever he spoke I found myself on the edge of my seat ready to object at a moment's notice.

Day after day the pace continued. My one-hour lunch break was merely a repetition of the early-morning hours. I conferred with detectives, attended to other cases and spoke briefly with the afternoon's prospective witnesses. The only thing that I never did find time to do during the luncheon recess was to eat lunch. It was no different after the trial had recessed for the day. At five o'clock I was back in my office with hours of work still left to do. In the evenings I waited for portions of the daily copy to be completed in order to review it, and then tried to step back and reflect on how things were going in general.

Usually I went home about 9 P.M., ate dinner and went directly to bed. I was not very good company while the trial was in progress. At night I found myself dreaming about it. Before it was over, I had lost more than twenty pounds.

The case played to a full house. I do not believe that anyone who wanted to observe it was ever turned away, but there were rarely many empty seats. Sooner or later almost everyone who worked in the courthouse stopped by to catch the show.

A small group of Richardson's young black supporters from Lincoln Hospital was there almost every day. At Lincoln Hospital mimeographed signs reading "Support James Richardson in His Hour of Need" were prominently displayed.

Across the aisle Pat Skagen sat all alone, in the first seat in the second row on the left. At the beginning of the trial Kunstler had requested that she not sit in the first row; he did not want the jury to guess the identity of the pretty young woman with the gray eyes.

The courtroom buffs were there too. Old pensioners, for the most part, the true aficionados of such proceedings, they are a breed apart. Whenever they are present, you can be sure that you are watching the most interesting trial in the courthouse. Even before the Richardson case began, a small entourage of buffs had begun to sit in on all of my trials. It was one of the signs that led me to feel I was becoming a pretty good trial lawyer. They were tough critics, veterans of thousands of performances, and knew their business well—better than some of the lawyers they observed. I felt good about their presence.

There was Al the Opera Singer, a frail, wispy-haired old man with a pink complexion and startling blue eyes. Once Al had been in the chorus of the Metropolitan Opera, and had traveled around the world. He never missed a day. Neither did Mabel, a little old woman who wore a nondescript knitted hat and faded cloth coat no matter what the weather. She carried a shopping bag and always wanted to see the defendant—any defendant—convicted.

Each morning I would ask Al, Mabel and the others for advice. Veteran jury watchers, they were wise and perceptive, and from them I learned what kind of impression I was making. They gave me confidence.

Most of the assistant district attorneys, Legal Aid lawyers and private attorneys who could spare a few moments in their schedules dropped in on the trial to see Kunstler. He had "made it big," and they wanted to see of what stuff fame is made. They came to learn.

One day Harry Belafonte appeared. He and Kunstler were friends. They had spoken about the case, and Belafonte had come to watch some of the trial, to see Kunstler and to meet James Richardson. When he arrived and I realized who he was, I was concerned. Would the jury recognize him as he sat with Richardson's supporters? Would it affect them? How could I prevent his presence from hurting my case? I had no answers to these questions.

During the morning recess, Kunstler introduced me to Belafonte and we chatted briefly. I learned that his daughter was at school in Williamstown, Massachusetts, in the same remote, beautiful Berkshire town where I had gone to school a decade earlier. I would have enjoyed talking with him longer, but not then. At the time, all I wanted was for him to get out of the courtroom. When he did not reappear after the luncheon recess, I was relieved.

My first witnesses were the civilians who had been in the subway station. I had given a great deal of thought to the order in which I would call witnesses. I had to begin with the civilians. Not only were they chronologically first in the narrative I wished to present, but they were essential to the tone I wished to establish. They were decent ordinary people, a hard-working cross section of Bronx County population, who I knew would be accepted by their peers on the jury.

First was Sylvester Farish, the sixty-three-year-old warehouseman who had been injured by a chip of flying cement that evening. He had put on his best suit for the occasion, and was obviously uncomfortable in it. I believe that the jury liked him for this; most of them would have felt the same way if they had been called upon to testify.

Farish's testimony was blunt and to the point. "When I went into the station . . . I saw a white man . . . with a white tee shirt and black pants chasing a colored fella on the station . . . He brought him up against the wall and told him to put his hands up against the wall . . . the next action I saw was the colored man come down and put his hands in his belt . . . [and move] counterclockwise. I heard a shot. The next thing I saw was them running through the gate here [indicating on the model and photographs]. The colored fellow first, and the guy with the white shirt right after. The man with the white shirt . . . pointed a gun at the stairs. I heard maybe two or three shots. Then . . . the man in the white shirt rolled down maybe three steps, rolled over onto his side."

"And did you notice anything with respect to your person?" I asked.

"Yes, afterwards . . . I looked at my arm and saw blood coming out. That's all I was interested in. I didn't bother with anything else."

By the time I sat down, my direct examination completed, there was little that Kunstler could do to effectively cross-examine Sylvester Farish. His testimony had been unadorned and patently true. There were no suspicious or unlikely details —only his real perceptions, distilled to their essence by the twenty-eight-month hiatus. If he had wished, Kunstler could have easily confused Farish by demonstrating that he had forgotten details, but he could never make a witness like this seem dishonest or mistaken in his testimony. Kunstler did not even try; to do so would only have antagonized the jury, and he was far too good a lawyer to do that. Instead, he merely asked Sylvester Farish a few gentle questions and then dismissed him.

Calvin Klinger, the token-booth clerk, was next. Balding, vacant-eyed and potbellied, wearing baggy pants and a V-necked sweater, he was dull, difficult, confused and inarticulate. His testimony had to be dragged out of him question by question. Yes, he had heard some shots. Yes, the subway station had been crowded. Yes, he had seen the man in the white "skibee" shirt fall by the staircase. It was like pulling teeth, and I could sense the jury losing patience with him. But before we were through, I did get one important piece of evidence out of Klinger. He recalled receiving from a bystander a blue leather case with a badge and James Richardson's identification papers. He could not recall the details, but he remembered that much. I placed the blue leather case and its contents into evidence.

Kunstler tore into Klinger on cross-examination. The witness was confused, to begin with, and under a steady stream of sharp questions he floundered. He was challenged on minor discrepancies between his testimony on trial and that which he had given to the grand jury. It was nothing serious, but he went to pieces, and admitted that he was mixed up and didn't remember anything very well. It was painful, and I'm sure everyone in the courtroom was relieved when he left the stand.

My next two witnesses were much better. Robert Jiminez, the high school student who had been helping his mother run the station newsstand, and Mrs. Betancourt, the office worker who had been on her way home, both made nice impressions as they described the incident briefly. They were clean-cut witnesses, and their testimony was straightforward. Kunstler barely bothered to cross-examine them. They were believed; there was no doubt in the jury's mind that there had been a confrontation between a black man and a white man that evening in the subway station. Shots had been fired, there had been a chase, and the white man had been gunned down near the stairs to the street.

Overall, the civilian testimony had been successful, and I

was pleased. But the real test lay ahead. There was no escaping the fact that my most important witnesses were all police officers. The shoot-out on the stairs, Richardson's apprehension, ballistics evidence and the confession all came from police testimony. Without police witnesses I had no case. Put another way, if the jury did not choose to believe these policemen, James Richardson would be acquitted; if they did, he would be convicted. It was as simple as that. This reality was not lost on Kunstler. At every possible opportunity throughout the voir dire he had made it clear that he viewed this case as a law enforcement conspiracy. He had promised the prospective jurors that he would establish this to their satisfaction. It was a promise that I could not afford to take lightly.

There was no conspiracy in the Richardson case. The evidence I was presenting was the truth as I had found it after a long, intensive investigation. Nothing was hidden, and no avenue of investigation had been left unexplored. Nevertheless, I knew that Kunstler would do his level best to make it seem otherwise, and I realized that a man of his abilities was quite capable of creating this illusion. He could easily make police witnesses seem dim-witted, confused, even pathetic. I could imagine him baiting witnesses, angering them and having them reveal hatreds or biases that would have a powerful impact on the jury. Such tactics might not change the fundamental testimony of a witness, but they certainly could change the way in which jurors might view it. I was concerned about the ability of these police officers to stand up to Kunstler's cross-examination.

Preparing a policeman for testimony is a different proposition than rehearsing a civilian. Sylvester Farish, Mrs. Betancourt and the other civilians had never testified before, so the prospect of being a witness, especially in a major murder case, was unique and disquieting. The goal in dealing with them was to help them avoid stage fright and panic, and to keep them relaxed so that they would tell their stories in their own words.

Police witnesses have to be approached from another perspective. The average officer is a seasoned witness and a trained observer who has been taught both to remember and to describe accurately what he has seen. Policemen are actually trained in how to give testimony, and this is reinforced a hundred times over by the practical experience of taking the stand and doing so. Any active police officer is at home on the witness stand. There are preliminary hearings in the Criminal Court, grand jury appearances and the trials themselves. Hence, there was no danger of my police witnesses suffering from stage fright. The trouble is that they are *too* seasoned. For them, taking the stand is merely an unpleasant task, a chore that they would sooner not have. They are so accustomed to testifying that they become blasé. They know that the defendant is guilty, and they don't quite see the need to go to all this trouble to convince twelve outsiders of the fact. Trials are generally boring to policemen, and they have a tendency to communicate this attitude to juries.

In addition, officers frequently pepper their testimony with clichés. Police jargon, usually unintelligible to lay jurors, is often employed. These men live in a work-oriented world, and they forget too easily that their listeners have not been initiated into the mysteries of police work. For instance, defendants are invariably and interchangeably referred to as "perpetrators," rather than by name. Crimes are referred to by their Penal Law section numbers, and time is given by the military system. The list is almost endless, for police talk is a dialect. Indeed, some officers actually need interpreters to make themselves understood. As a result, police testimony ends up sounding like a script written by an unimaginative committee and memorized from some manual. It sounds as if it were composed to be applicable, without variation, to all robberies or all rapes or all murders. I have seen juries emphatically reject such testimony even when it was sincerely and truthfully given. Some jurors simply refuse to believe that an honest person would give testimony in such a way.

Another serious problem with police testimony is one which each year has become more and more severe—that of credibility. Every headline, every newscast and every exposé revealing a new instance of police corruption, brutality or misconduct makes this problem worse. Today the general credibility of law enforcement officials is at an all-time low. The Knapp commission, Watergate and the congressional investigations into the FBI and CIA have served to lower public regard for law enforcement, and it is now popular to take the cynical position that all cops are bums, and that none of them are worthy of belief.

The truth of the matter is that policemen are human beings endowed with the same innate capacity for virtue or vice as most other men. Certainly, some officers are vicious and even pathological liars. Others are rigidly honest, even in their most minor dealings. The majority, like most of the rest of us, fall somewhere in between. A badge and a gun is no guarantee that a man will tell the truth, but neither is it a guarantee that he will lie.

I worried that some jurors might hold the latter view, and I was sure that Kunstler would exploit this if it existed, so I had spent hours preparing my police witnesses to testify. It was not a question of going over *what* they had to say and refreshing their recollections; they all remembered June 28, 1972, well enough. My primary interest was in *how* they would testify. I wanted them to focus on the jury, to look at them and, above all, to speak directly to them. Over and over I stressed that they were not to use jargon. People were to be referred to by their names, and they should speak plain, everyday English. I also warned them about Kunstler. I didn't want any of them to fall into any traps. I stressed that they were not to argue politics with him and that they were not to lose their tempers, regardless of the provocation. Treat the defense attorney with courtesy. If he is rude or hostile, remember that it will hurt his side, not ours, in the jury's eyes.

With the police witnesses the confessions seemed to be the

place to begin. Logically, they were a link that connected the civilian testimony with what followed, and they gave the jury a fuller picture of what had happened in the subway station. The confessions were a strong element of my case; they had already been tested during the Huntley Hearing and had stood up. I knew that they would hurt Richardson badly.

Luis Cruz, the Transit Police detective, took the stand. I expected him to be my best witness. He is a particularly bright and articulate man, and as seems to be true of a substantial number of the Puerto Rican police officers I have met, he is dedicated to the idea of self-improvement. At the time of the trial he was in the process of applying to law schools. He had obtained his college degree at night while serving as a police officer, and it was his intention to do the same for a law degree. Cruz is one of those rare individuals who can bridge the gap between a South Bronx slum and a college classroom; he would feel right at home in either. I knew that he would make a good impression on the jury. The fact that he was Puerto Rican did not hurt; Kunstler's racist-conspiracy theory would seem a lot less likely with witnesses like Luis Cruz, Frank Santiago or Hank Arana.

Once on the stand, Cruz repeated the testimony he had given two weeks earlier during the pre-trial hearing. I asked him to identify Richardson. He did so, turning in his seat and looking Richardson right in the eye: "It's the gentleman sitting right there [pointing], by the gentleman with the glasses [indicating Kunstler]." As always, there was something electric about an identification in court. One or two jurors nodded as Cruz identified Richardson as the man who had confessed.

Then Cruz told the jury of the defendant's confession. They all leaned forward to listen; they wanted to hear what Richardson had said to the "Spanish detective." He told them of the confrontation as the defendant had described it. You could envision the two men with their guns out: Skagen firing the first shot, the groin wound, and Richardson firing back.

Cruz described both the prisoner's concern that he was being charged with a robbery and his second confession for the purpose of setting the record straight. The handwritten notes the detective had scribbled that night were placed in evidence and were read to the jury.

Kunstler was surprisingly gentle with Cruz. He questioned him on his skills as a stenographer, and established that his notes were not a verbatim rendition of the confession he had heard. He brought out the fact that Cruz had not bothered to have Richardson read and sign the notes he had written down. He scored some minor points during his cross-examination, but not many. What surprised me was the tone of his questions. They were not challenging, and he did not give the impression that he thought that Cruz was lying.

Detective Richard Gest of the 8th Homicide Assault Squad was next. He told the jury of the confession he had heard, and read his notes to them. They were in question-and-answer form.

"Where do you live?"

"720 Hunts Point Avenue."

"Where do you work?"

"Lincoln Hospital, as a senior admitting clerk."

"What happened this afternoon?"

"At about five P.M. I was on my way to work. I was late and I called in. Should have been there at four P.M. After I bought a token I went through the turnstile and this white man came over and we had words."

"What words?"

"Asked me my name, where I was going and for identification."

"Why you of all people?"

"Probably saw my gun stuck inside my trousers."

"Then what happened?"

"I got mad and cursed. Then he pulled out his badge and gun and backed up and fired one shot at me."

"Where did this bullet hit you?"

"In the right groin."

"Then what?"

"I pulled out my gun and fired at him, and then I ran."

"What kind of gun did you have?"

"A thirty-two caliber nickel-plated snub nose."

"Then what?"

"I ran upstairs and was jumped by a big cop in uniform."

"Then what?"

"I broke away and ran across the street where I was caught."

"What happened to the gun?"

"I threw it over the fence just before being caught."

Detective Gest is a man of medium build with thinning blond hair. Throughout the pre-trial investigation and hearing he had sported a modest goatee, but a week before the trial he had shaved it off. He had done this on his own; no one had suggested it.

Kunstler took one look at Gest and went right to work.

Q. Detective Gest, you testified in a preliminary hearing in this case, did you not, last week, I believe?

A. That is correct.

Q. Or the week before, I guess, and at that time you were wearing a beard, were you not?

A. That is correct.

Q. When did you shave your beard?

A. After the first hearing.

Q. Did you shave it in preparation for this trial?

A. No.

Q. Did you receive any instructions to shave it?

A. None.

Q. Was it your decision to shave it?

A. That is correct.

It was a neat way to begin a cross-examination. It was unexpected and caught everyone off guard. With a few short questions, sharply put, Kunstler had succeeded in creating the impression that perhaps this witness was trying to change his appearance in order to make a more favorable impression on the jury. Without asking a single substantive question about the detective's testimony, Kunstler had succeeded in casting the shadow of a doubt on his reliability. It was a masterly beginning, but the rest of the cross-examination did not live up to its early promise. It was a somewhat more hostile replay of the questions he had asked earlier of Detective Cruz, and it did not get far.

Kunstler closed with a single question, which came out of the blue and was totally unrelated to those that had preceded it. As he was returning to his seat he suddenly turned to Detective Gest and asked, "Was Patrolman Wieber indicted for this crime?" I was on my feet in an instant. "Your Honor . . ." I began, but before I could go further, Justice Warner had reacted: "Sustained! Strike it out! The jury will disregard the question!" Of course, they could not disregard the question, for they had heard Kunstler ask it. They could not be expected to erase it from their memories. I could only hope that it would not take their minds off what Detective Gest had told them. The time to answer that last question would come later.

The following morning Patrolman Frank Santiago took the stand. He was a transitional witness between the confession and the apprehension, for he was the officer who had actually caught Richardson after the chase. He had also transported the defendant to Lincoln Hospital, stood guard over him, and witnessed or participated in all of the questioning. With the exception of Wieber and Jacobsen, he was on the stand longer than any other witness.

Santiago is a handsome young officer who projects an open, cheerful personality. Although he was relatively inexperienced and had spent little time on the witness stand, after a few minutes it seemed as if he had been born there. He handled himself beautifully, always talking to the jurors and always making sense.

Using the blown up aerial photographs that I had obtained of the streets around the Hunt's Point station, I had Santiago describe the case that led to Richardson's arrest. These photographs permitted the jury to envision the chase easily. Santiago also described the statements by the defendant to the friends and relatives who had visited him and asked what had happened. He gave the jury a detailed description of what it had been like at Lincoln Hospital that night: the confusion, with all the police and medical personnel coming and going. He portrayed the scene graphically and in perspective.

Kunstler spent a great deal of time cross-examining Santiago, but got nowhere.

May Elaine Williams took the stand next. I had not intended to call her at this point, but she seemed nervous while sitting in my office waiting her turn. I did not want her to brood while the lengthy police evidence was presented, so I decided to call her at the first possible opportunity.

As is often the case with witnesses who dread the prospect of taking the stand, Mrs. Williams was fine once she actually began to testify. Her nervousness vanished and she became her natural self, a solid, sensible woman. Her testimony was brief and to the point. She told of her employment as a correction guard and her departure from the job, and of the fact that she had been issued a gold correction officer's shield, which she had kept after she quit. Then she told the jury that she had been working as a barmaid at Marzan's Bar during the spring of 1972, and that her purse had disappeared from the bar on March 2, 1972. I did not dare ask her to mention the robbery that day; I was concerned that any reference, brought out by my questioning, to a crime that the defendant was not charged with, might lead to the declaration of a mistrial. Richardson was not charged with the robbery, and so I avoided all references to it.

Mrs. Williams then told of the telegram she had received, and of her meeting with a man who called himself James Richardson.

Q. Now, Mrs. Williams, did you have a conversation with that man who identified himself as James Richardson?

A. Yes.

Q. And will you tell us what [was said]?

A. I thanked him for returning my identification . . . I noticed that my badge was missing, and I asked him where the badge was, and he said that that was the way that he found it.

Q. Now, Mrs. Williams, did you ever give that man permission or authority to take . . . your badge and leather case?

A. No, I didn't.

As I asked these questions the jury looked at Richardson. Mrs. Williams could not positively identify him as the man she had met, but as she produced the telegram and read the part about Richardson and Lincoln Hospital, some jurors gave each other knowing looks. When she identified the badge and blue leather case that Calvin Klinger had found at the scene of the shooting, the point was made. It was damning testimony that put Richardson in a very bad light.

The thrust of Kunstler's cross-examination of Mrs. Williams was to establish that on March 2, 1972, she was no longer a corrections officer. As she had on direct examination, she admitted freely that she had been negligent in not returning the badge when she had quit her job at Bedford Hills. Strictly speaking, she had not been the lawful owner of that badge on March 2, 1972. Having made this point, Kunstler asked for permission to approach the side bar. Outside the hearing of the jury, he asked that the seventh count of the indictment, charging Richardson with the possession of stolen property, be dismissed. He argued that since on March 2, 1972, Mrs. Williams had not been the lawful owner of the badge and leather case, her testimony could not lawfully establish the charge.

It was a weak argument, and had no true foundation in law.

I had foreseen this line of attack and was ready for it. There is a well-established principle in criminal law that the crimes of larceny and criminal possession of stolen property can victimize anybody who has possession of an object, and not merely those who have legal title to it. I argued that the technical niceties of Mrs. William's possession of the badge were irrelevant. What mattered was that so far as James Richardson knew, she *was* the owner. He had no right to dispute her title to the badge, and if he knowingly deprived her of its use—notwithstanding the fact that she was no longer a corrections officer—he was guilty.

Justice Warner listened patiently to our arguments and made up his mind on the spot. "It seems to me, Mr. Kunstler, that she [Mrs. Williams] had the responsibility for the whereabouts of that badge, even though she should have returned it . . . and if someone else comes along and deprives her of that responsibility . . . this badge should not be kept from her . . ."

MR. KUNSTLER: Judge, I'm not even . . . saying that, but the indictment must be read strictly.

JUSTICE WARNER: I'm going to deny your application at this time.

MR. KUNSTLER: Okay.

JUSTICE WARNER: However, I would give both counsel opportunity before the case is submitted to the jury to submit a memorandum.

The judge had ruled in my favor, as I knew he would. I suspected that Kunstler would not bother to submit a memorandum on this point. I was right; he never did.

Kunstler returned to his cross-examination of Mrs. Williams and immediately got himself into trouble.

Q. Did you ever report to the Department of Corrections that the shield was missing?
A. I reported it to the police.
Q. You reported it to the police?
A. Yes.

Q. When did you do that?
A. On the date that my identification was missing, the bar had been held up, and the police were there, and I reported it to one of the policemen.

On his own, Kunstler had brought out the fact that Marzan's Bar had been robbed. Again a few jurors looked at one another knowingly. I was delighted. Kunstler could not complain that I had prejudiced his client's case; he had done so himself, by asking Mrs. Williams an open-ended question to which he had not known the answer. When he got the answer, it hurt his case.

Mrs. Williams left the stand shortly thereafter. From my point of view, her testimony had been a triumph.

The ballistics men, the doctors and the medical examiner all testified in turn. In rapid succession, they all informed the jury of their expertise, training and many years of practical experience. Experts make impressive witnesses; they come cloaked in their special wisdom, and jurors are inclined to respect and believe them. I noticed that most of the male jurors leaned forward and paid great attention to the ballistics men. I had seen this before. Firearms have an irresistible fascination for the American male. In a sense, this was what the case was all about. James Richardson had had no business carrying a gun that afternoon. Perhaps he had done so because guns were fascinating to him as well. Now, as the experts spoke of twists and calibers and lands and grooves, I could see interest mounting in the eyes of the male jurors.

I was deliberately repetitive in eliciting the medical and ballistics testimony, for I wanted to hammer into the jury's consciousness the facts that would lead them to the conclusion that Richardson had fired first. I had the doctors demonstrate the paths that the various bullets had taken through Skagen's and Richardson's bodies, and I had the ballistics men take the jurors step by step through the tests to their conclusions. I hoped that this testimony had sunk in. The burden of tying it all up cohesively would rest with me during summation.

Next I put Raul Bianchi on the stand. He testified about the .32 caliber Clerke he had found in the railroad yard on the evening of June 28, 1972; he described the gun and told how he had taken it home and unloaded it in his backyard. Of the five shells in the gun, one was alive and the other four were spent. He had thrown them all in the garbage.

I asked Bianchi what he had done with the gun.

A. I sold it.
Q. And where did you sell that gun?
A. Fox Street.
Q. And how much did you get . . .
A. Sixty-five dollars.
Q. And what did you do with the sixty-five dollars?
A. I spent them. I bought shoes.

The jury laughed.

Kunstler did not bother to cross-examine Bianchi at any length, which surprised me. Bianchi was vulnerable to cross-examination; he was inarticulate, and could easily be cast in a light unattractive to some jurors. Instead, Kunstler merely asked the witness whether he had been threatened with arrest by Detective Arana for possession of the gun he had sold.

There were other street-wise witnesses to put on the stand: the four teenagers who had been hanging around the Hunts Point station that afternoon. Some of them had seen the shoot-out and the chase on the street, and so, dressed in blue jeans, sneakers and T-shirts, they testified. Loose and easygoing, they did not give a damn that they were appearing in a major trial. They had never heard of William Kunstler, and they were not impressed with him or me or the judge. As nearly as I could tell, the only one they did respect, and like, was Hank Arana, the detective who had brought them to court.

Since their importance was limited, they were on the stand

briefly. A black man with a gun in his hand had been running from a bunch of cops. The jury had heard all this before; the real significance of this testimony was simply its source. These witnesses were as different from police officers as you could expect to find, hardly the stuff of which a government conspiracy could be built, and yet they were corroborating in many particulars the details of police testimony. Their observations would make it more difficult for the defense to argue its conspiracy theory.

Kunstler treated these witnesses with kindness and sympathy. It was clear that he would have been far more comfortable defending them, and he had no stomach for discrediting them. In the case of one witness in particular, this attitude became clear in an interesting exchange.

At the outset of the trial, I had given Kunstler all the arrest and conviction records of the witnesses I intended to call during the trial. This was a routine procedure that would permit him to cross-examine them about their prior criminal acts in order to discredit their testimony. Just before one of these youngsters took the stand, I learned that he had recently gotten into some serious trouble. Consequently, after I finished questioning him, I asked to approach the side bar, and outside the jury's hearing I informed the judge and Kunstler of this new development.

Kunstler replied, "My policy is never to use convictions unless they go to the question of perjury or politically . . . I'm against the use of these [criminal records] even though I know I have a right to do it. I . . . prefer for my own political background not to go into [this]. I'm going to ask my client, because I think I have an obligation to . . . but I think he will follow my dictates. I don't think this is ethical to do, even though it may somehow be legal."

Obviously embarrassed and on the spot, Kunstler was not speaking clearly. In effect, he was saying that because of a personally held political belief he would refuse an opportunity to damage my case. James Richardson was on trial for murder, facing the awful possibility of life imprisonment. A witness had given damaging testimony, and Richardson's attorney had an opportunity to compromise the man in the eyes of the jurors. Once they heard about the witness's criminal record, they would be far less likely to believe him. Knowing this, Kunstler nevertheless refused to press his advantage.

Kunstler was on questionable grounds in taking this position. He had an obligation to do everything lawful within his power to win an acquittal for his client. Neither the sincerity nor the delicacy of his private political philosophy would make it any easier for Richardson to serve a life sentence, and Kunstler had no business representing the defendant if he was not prepared to do everything legally possible to win an acquittal. A Gandhi or a Berrigan might properly take such a position; for after all, it is he as the defendant who will suffer the consequences if convicted. A defense attorney does not have the same luxury.

However, as Kunstler predicted, after a few seconds of discussion Richardson agreed not to ask the question. The trial went on.

There was no denying the fact that the dramatic high point of my case would be the testimony of Patrolmen Pade, Rath, Jacobsen and, above all, Wieber. As time went on and the other elements of my case were admitted in evidence with surprising ease, it became clear that Kunstler was saving his fire for these officers. I cautioned them before they took the stand to remain civil, and to be absolutely candid in answering Kunstler's questions.

It began with John Jacobsen. "Jake," as he is known, is a tall man with blond hair, a long face and Scandinavian features. A long-time police officer and veteran of the 41st Precinct, he had seen it all. His face revealed this. He was no stranger to personal tragedy. Sometime before the trial (but after the shooting), his wife had been killed in an automobile accident, leaving him with young children to raise. He had borne this blow and faced his responsibilities squarely. One could sense the man's quiet determination.

Jacobsen testified that he had been issuing a summons to a flower peddler when he heard shots coming from the subway station. He told how Richardson had run up the stairs shouting, "Someone is shooting! Someone is shooting!" He described Skagen, in civilian clothing with his gun out, at the bottom of the stairs, and stated that he had not known that Skagen was a police officer. He had heard a shot and had attempted to stop Richardson to discover what was going on.

I asked Jacobsen whether it was his intention to arrest Richardson, and he answered no, that he had only wanted information.

Q. Officer Jacobsen, will you tell us what happened next?
A. Defendant Richardson broke free, [and] I went sprawling into the street.
Q. Now, when you say "broke free," describe as precisely as you can how he broke free.
A. He shook me off. I went on my backside into the street and when I started to recover myself, I observed . . . Richardson with a gun in his hand, pointing [it] in my direction.
Q. Now will you describe, as best you can, the gun that you observed in [his] hand?
A. A chrome-plated revolver.

I took Jacobsen through the chase, the gun going over the fence, and the apprehension, and then turned him over to Kunstler.

The cross-examination was savage. Kunstler made it quite clear that he did not like this big white cop and went over his testimony step by step, seeking to portray him as a bloodthirsty beast.

Q. . . . did you fire a shot at him [Richardson]?
A. I did.
Q. Did you shoot to kill?

A. I shot at the defendant.
Q. Did you shoot to kill him?
A. No.
Q. Did you shoot to injure him?
A. I wanted to stop him.
Q. What part of his body did you shoot at?
A. His body.
Q. When you say his body, do you mean . . . the point between his hips and his shoulders?
A. That's the largest part.
Q. And you wanted to put a bullet in that part of the body, did you not?
A. It [was] the only way I saw at that time to stop him.
Q. When you were shooting at him, he wasn't even pointing a gun at you, was he?
A. He stopped and pointed in my direction a second time.
Q. When you shot he was running, wasn't he?
A. He paused and pointed in my direction and I let go a round at that time.

It was an effective cross-examination. What Kunstler did not ask, and what Jacobsen was not permitted to explain, was that a police revolver is a highly inaccurate weapon, especially at a distance, and that police officers are trained to aim for the largest part of their target. The public is conditioned to seeing the white hats in horse operas shoot guns out of the hands of the black hats and perform other amazing feats of marksmanship with six-shooters. In real life it does not work that way. You cannot aim a revolver as you would a rifle; all you can do is to point it, fire and hope for the best.

Kunstler's real point, of course, was that Jacobsen, Wieber and all the other police officers were a trigger-happy lot who shot first and asked questions later. Without explicitly saying so, this was the explanation that he was offering to the jury for the tragedy that had occurred. It was a powerful argument, and I knew that I would have to answer it. I decided that I would save my rebuttal for summation.

Kunstler went on.

Q. . . . as I understand your testimony, you fired a total of three shots?

A. Correct.

Q. At James Richardson?

A. That's correct.

Q. Up to . . . the time you fired the last two shots, you didn't know whether he [had] committed any crimes, did you?

A. Yes, I did.

Q. You knew he committed a crime?

A. Yes.

Q. What crime did he commit?

A. I felt he attempted to murder me.

Q. He . . . attempted to murder you?

A. Correct.

Q. When he didn't fire a shot at you?

A. He pointed a gun at me. As far as I was concerned, the gun was loaded.

The cross-examination seemed to continue interminably Kunstler asked Jacobsen many questions about George Wieber, the point of which was to suggest to the jury that Wieber was the true criminal in this case. Jacobsen proved to be a game witness. He answered Kunstler's questions forthrightly, and followed my advice of remaining civil in the face of obvious hostility. As a result, though he was embarrassed by Kunstler and at times was made to look unpleasant, by the second day of the grilling a change in the atmosphere occurred. Jacobsen was answering questions so straightforwardly that it became evident to all that he was being absolutely sincere and truthful. He was not ducking tough questions, but was answering promptly and responsively, even if the answers occasionally made him look bad. Throughout the entire cross-examination, which lasted eight hours, he never budged from his account. By some strange alchemy, in time he began to earn the respect of the people in the courtroom simply by telling the unadorned truth, regardless of the consequences. This was not lost on the jury, and even Kunstler during his summation was to acknowledge this by complimenting Jacobsen for his candor.

Patrolmen Pade and Rath also testified, and were cross-examined by Kunstler in much the same fashion. Their ordeals were much briefer, since essentially their testimony corroborated Jacobsen's. Nobody was interested in going over the same ground ad nauseam. Besides, everyone was waiting for George Wieber to take the stand.

25

George Wieber

John Skagen was dead. The jury would never see his face nor hear his voice, but he was a specter that haunted the trial. Without appearance or personality, he became a kind of disembodied idea as the trial progressed. He was everyman, senselessly killed and prematurely in his grave.

If John Skagen was a specter, James Richardson was a sphinx. Each morning he took a seat at the counsel table, and throughout the day's proceedings would sit, staring forward, mute and expressionless. Whatever thoughts and emotions he experienced were not revealed; he permitted others to recount his deeds, to repeat his words, and to speculate about his motives. As a man, he, too, remained a mystery. Though he was a physical presence at the trial who had substance, he, too, was without personality.

It fell to a third man, George Wieber, to bring the trial fully to life. On his shoulders alone rested the burden of reliving the memory of the fatal encounter that linked him to both Skagen and Richardson. One man had died; a second had been seriously injured, imprisoned, and was on trial facing a life sentence. The third, Wieber, was physically untouched, had been cleared of all charges and was freely pursuing his career. Yet Wieber was as much a victim of the Hunts Point subway shooting as were the other two. A man must live with his memories. And for George Wieber, the trial of James Richardson was an ordeal that had loomed for almost three years.

You would not notice George Wieber in a crowd. Of average height and build, he has dark hair and sad brown eyes. He wears his police uniform well, and his manner is mild. He is a sympathetic person and a good listener. No one would ever cast him for the role he had played at Hunts Point that day.

Wieber is also a good cop whose entire career has been spent working tough precincts. He has worked them well, and has never shirked the difficult or unpleasant jobs. While others went in for glamorous assignments, the undercover or detective work that catches attention, Wieber kept to his patrol duties on the front lines quietly and steadily, dealing with each emergency as it arose. He saw it all—family disputes, street fights, medical emergencies—and always there was no time to prepare. They happened, something had to be done, and he did it quietly and efficiently, without the luxury of a moment to reflect or debate. Patrol work is incredibly difficult to do well, but Wieber does it well. He and the men like him are the backbone of any police department.

I came to know and like George Wieber in the many hours we spent in my office preparing for his testimony. It could not have been easy for him; over and over again he was forced to relive those few seconds when he had made the fatal decision to fire his gun at the man at the bottom of the stairs, a decision that he had been second-guessing for three years.

Doubts had plagued Wieber from the beginning. At the 41st Precinct that night, all of the investigators, detectives, brass and the assistant district attorney had given him the third degree. What had he done? Didn't he know that Skagen was a cop? Dazed, he had answered the questions mechanically, thinking only about the fact that a mile away, at Lincoln Hospital, the man he had shot, a brother officer, was fighting for his life. Wieber did not know then Richardson had also shot Skagen; he believed he had done it all.

At ten o'clock, word filtered back to the precinct that Skagen had died. When Wieber was told, he got up without a word, walked into the bathroom and threw up. He came back into the squad room and broke into sobs. No one said a word. A short time later they sent him home.

The weeks that followed were bad. There was the publicity and the sidelong glances from the other cops in the precinct, each of them wearing the black bands of mourning for a fellow officer killed in the line of duty. Wieber wore one over his badge like the other officers, and put one over the wooden grip of his service revolver. He never removed the latter; to this day, it is still there.

John Skagen was given the obligatory inspector's funeral, and as always, delegations of police officers from all over the metropolitan area attended. Wieber was advised not to attend the funeral; his appearance was not considered proper. But he did attend the grand jury inquest; there was no avoiding it. It was there that the strain began to show. He was sitting in Bill Quinn's office getting ready to testify and to sign his waiver of immunity, and was being questioned for what seemed the millionth time. Suddenly he unpinned the badge from his chest and threw it on the desk. He said to Bill Quinn, "I don't want to be a cop anymore. Take the badge," and buried his face in his hands.

Quinn calmed Wieber down. They talked some, and Bill persuaded him that he was being foolish.

George Wieber once told me that he did not know what he would have done during this period without his wife. Her love and understanding braced him to face the ordeals that followed. At the time of his testimony at the trial, Wieber was on the verge of becoming a father for the first time, and was excited and apprehensive. Perhaps it was fitting that in the same week he would both close and open important chapters of his life.

I'd had to introduce George Wieber to Pat Skagen. It was an inevitable meeting, for both of them were clearly going to spend a lot of time around my office, and they could hardly be expected to ignore each other. They shook hands and looked at each other, without a word. We were all stiff and uncomfortable; there was nothing anyone could say. We had only one common purpose that tied us together: the desire to see James Richardson successfully prosecuted.

For the final time, George Wieber was telling his story in a soft voice to the jury. We took it slowly, step by step, in a silent courtroom.

Q. Now, how old are you?
A. I'll be 33 next month.
Q. Are you married?
A. Yes, I am.
Q. And have you any children?
A. Next week I'll have one.

This broke the ice and some jurors smiled. It made Wieber human; they could relate to him.

We moved on to the heart of his testimony: he was issuing a summons to a peddler outside the subway when there were three or four shots inside the station.

Q. Now, when you heard these sounds, will you tell us what . . . you heard or saw next?
A. I saw people coming up out of the subway station, people screaming, and I heard someone yell, "There's a crazy man down there shooting at us!"

Q. What happened then?

A. I was proceeding down the steps to the subway platform when a man came around the corner—the gun pointing up. I heard a shot. It appeared to me to be a shot. I saw a slight amount of smoke, and I thought the man was shooting at me and I fired at him.

Q. And do you know how many times you fired your gun?

A. At that time no, but later on [I learned that] it was six times.

Q. And how many shots does your gun hold?

A. Six.

Q. Now after you fired those shots did you see the man in the black shirt do anything?

A. Yes, he fell.

Q. . . . what [did you do] then?

A. I ran down and took his gun and put it in my pocket, and I ran past him to see if there was anyone else shooting or if anybody else was hurt.

Q. . . . did there come a time . . . when you went back to the man who was on the ground?

A. Yes, I went immediately back to him and he stated to me, "I'm on the job," and he put his hand in his pocket and pulled out his shield.

Q. Will you tell us what in police jargon the phrase, "I'm on the job" means?

A. That means he's a police officer.

"I'm on the job" were the last words John Skagen ever spoke. In the audience Pat Skagen heard every word of George Wieber's testimony, but she never lost her composure.

I wrapped up my direct examination quickly. Wieber told of his trip to Lincoln Hospital, then of being ordered back to the 41st Precinct, where he was questioned over and over by dozens of detectives and was advised of his constitutional rights.

Q. And how were you feeling during that evening?

A. Sick to my stomach.

Q. And did there come a time when you learned that John Skagen had died?
A. Yes.
Q. Do you recall [what] you did at that time?
A. Yes.
Q. . . what . . .?
A. I cried.

Justice Warner declared a ten-minute recess after Wieber's testimony. We all needed it.

Kunstler should not have asked George Wieber a single question. The witness had said it all; there was nothing more to ask. His testimony had not hurt Richardson; he had very little to say about the defendant. They had passed each other for a split second, and Wieber had heard someone shout, "There's a crazy man down there shooting at us." He could not even identify who had spoken. Further, Wieber had admitted that he had emptied his gun at John Skagen. The jury had heard and would not forget.

But Kunstler could not resist the opportunity to harass Wieber. What he hoped to accomplish was unclear, but I could see that he relished this opportunity to torment a cop. He made Wieber repeat every detail of his testimony over and over.

Wieber complied. His voice became softer and softer, but he answered each question directly and everyone could hear his answers. I believe that this cross-examination was a blunder. George Wieber was a sympathetic figure to everyone in that courtroom. We all could detect his grief over Skagen's death, and the black band of mourning that he wore was indisputably sincere. Yet here was Kunstler, with a smile on his face, deliberately prolonging the agony. We all endured it silently except for George Wieber, who spoke softly.

Wieber's testimony ended on an explosion of anger between myself and Kunstler. He had been discussing various peripheral matters when suddenly he shifted tack.

Q. Now, you indicated that when you found out that police officer Skagen had died that you cried, remember that?
A. Yes.

Suddenly Kunstler raised his voice and snarled, "Did you cry when Clifford Glover and . . ."

I reacted quickly. Clifford Glover was a black youth who had been shot and killed by a police officer in a notorious and controversial incident a year earlier, and Kunstler had no right to interject that incident into this case. I screamed at the top of my lungs in an effort to stop him before he could say another word. It was the first time in the trial that I had raised my voice, and it worked. Kunstler was so startled that he shut up.

MR. PHILLIPS: I OBJECT!!
THE COURT: HOLD IT!
MR. PHILLIPS: I OBJECT!!
THE COURT: Hold it, Mr. Kunstler. Just one minute, please. Mr. Kunstler, let's have a conference in the robing room with the reporter.

In the robing room I was steaming.

MR. KUNSTLER: Judge, I think the crying is a fraud on his part . . . I don't believe that he cried.
THE COURT: It may very well be, Mr. Kunstler, but that is absolutely no excuse for your asking him what you asked him.
MR. KUNSTLER: Judge, if he cried at this accidental happening and did not cry when a young black kid was shot to death on the streets of Brooklyn and Queens, I think the jury can take that as probative that he might be telling an untruth.
THE COURT: Mr. Kunstler, it has absolutely nothing to do with this case and you know it!

Kunstler was being sincere; he simply could not bring himself to understand or believe Wieber had cried when he learned that John Skagen was dead. It had been a tragic mistake. Of course George Wieber had cried. What man wouldn't? As to Clifford Glover, Wieber had not shot him. He had read about it in the newspaper, just as everyone else had. Where was the comparison?

Kunstler had revealed himself. In the final analysis, he had shown that he did not realize that George Wieber was a human being. To Kunstler he was just a cop, a hated enemy, a pig—not only the man who shot Skagen but also the one who had shot Clifford Glover. Perhaps all cops look alike to Kunstler; certainly he was denying them their humanity.

I could only hope that the jury had not fallen for Kunstler's aborted outburst. I had faith that they would see it for what it was, but still I worried. The answer would come only with the verdict.

When Wieber left the stand the day was over and the two of us returned to my office. George was about to leave—he was to resume his normal duties the following day—when Pat Skagen entered. As he said goodbye to both of us, Pat looked at him and said, "George, you go home tonight and don't worry about me. I'll be okay, so don't worry." Then she gave him a little kiss on the cheek.

Wieber's eyes filled up and he left.

I turned to Pat Skagen. "I'm glad you did that," I said.

She looked levelly at me. "I wanted to say that to him. I saw what he had gone through, and I wanted to say it."

26

The People Rest

At 4:30 P.M. on October 15, 1974, I rested the People's case. I had called twenty-three witnesses to the stand; forty exhibits had been marked into evidence; and eight hundred and fifty-nine pages of testimony had been transcribed. I might have done more, but I knew that if I was unable to prove my case with my main witnesses, I would never be able to do so with an endless repetition of peripheral trivia. It felt good to say "The People rest." I was confident that I had done well.

At the end of the prosecution's case, defense counsel moves as a matter of course for the dismissal of the indictment for failure to prove a prima facie case. This means that the defense contends that the prosecution, even if believed by the jury in every respect, has failed to establish all the elements of the crimes charged. It is a *pro forma* motion and is generally made for the purpose of preserving certain issues for possible appellate review. Ninety-nine times out of a hundred it is denied without much ceremony.

But there was nothing *pro forma* about this case, and nothing *pro forma* about this motion to dismiss. I had spent many hours in the law library preparing to defend the propriety of this indictment from attack, and had labored over a lengthy memorandum of law, written in anticipation of this motion, which I had submitted to the court and to Kunstler at the beginning of the trial.

The jury was sent from the courtroom. Kunstler had not prepared a reply memorandum, and as he rose to speak I was apprehensive. He'd had weeks to study my memorandum and prepare a response, and there was certainly a great deal that he could say to denigrate my novel legal theory in support of the homicide counts of the indictment. I was afraid that he might unleash some powerful and persuasive argument that would persuade Justice Warner to throw out the indictment—and I had no doubt that if so persuaded, he would not hesitate to dismiss the case.

But Kunstler had prepared no memorandum. Though he argued at length, not once did he cite any applicable case law. I was relieved, but in a way I felt cheated. He began by asserting that there had been no proof of felony murder for the simple reason that there had been no proof of an underlying escape. He went on to claim that there was no proof that John Skagen had ever identified himself as a police officer or had taken out his shield.

This was too much for the judge, who interrupted: "Excuse me for cutting you off. How about the defendant's alleged statements that the police officer pulled out his gun and shield?"

Kunstler hemmed and hawed. "Well, your Honor, I don't think that—I was going to get to the statements in a moment —I don't think the statements by themselves, even though you have admitted them, of course you haven't got the medical testimony, again in this record during the trial—but I don't think the statements are the evidence which should furnish the escape . . . in the second degree or the felony murder. The word 'shield' occurs . . . in the big statement which is not before your Honor. It may occur in some of those smaller statements, I'm not sure. I haven't looked at them . . ."

I couldn't believe that Kunstler had not bothered to look at the confessions that his client had made. Fortunately, the court and everyone else had. Legally, Kunstler's arguments had no merit. Confessions are perfectly acceptable evidence and always have been. Many people have been convicted on the basis of little more than a believed confession, and many more will be in the future.

Later Kunstler would argue to the jury quite effectively that the "confessions" should be rejected as unbelievable fabrications invented by the police to convict his client. But when he made these arguments to Justice Warner, he was only wasting his breath. The court was not the judge of the facts; the jury was. For purposes of the motion, the court had to treat my proof, including the confession, as if the jury would believe it all. Nevertheless, Kunstler went on at length attacking the credibility of my evidence; in effect, he was delivering his summation.

Next, Kunstler expressed the opinion that "felony murder was unconstitutional." Where he got this idea from I don't know. He could cite no authority for the proposition, simply because there is none. He made no argument in support of this contention; it was merely a bald assertion.

He continued with the argument that since no gun belonging to Richardson had been produced, the weapon count should be dismissed. A first-year law student would have been publicly shamed by his professor had he argued such an absurd position, and I could not help wondering as I listened what Justice Warner was thinking about his former professor.

I had not warned Pat Skagen about the motion to dismiss and what it meant. It had taken her by surprise, and listening to Kunstler earnestly argue that the indictment should be thrown out was almost more than she could take. She practically jumped out of her seat, her eyes flashing fire. She looked as if she were ready to kill somebody, and did not calm down until I began to speak.

I was keyed up, ready to respond to Kunstler's arguments. It turned out that he had said nothing that really required a serious answer. My written memorandum was more than enough to deal with the points he had raised, so I could have stood mute and relied upon it. But I could not resist indulging myself and articulating my arguments. I showed off my forensic skills and had a good time doing so in a rush of words. I could sense that the judge understood exactly what I was saying.

I argued the propriety of the indictment count by count. The possession of the stolen badge had been proved. I reminded him of the telegram a James Richardson had sent to Mrs. Williams. The badge had been found on the scene; Richardson's ID was with it and he had known that the badge belonged to Mrs. Williams. There was plenty of evidence to support a conviction on this count.

The same was true of the gun. I mentioned the witnesses who had seen Richardson with the gun, those who had heard the shots, and the ballistics evidence. I reminded the judge of the efforts to track down the gun and of the defendant's confessions.

On and on I went, reiterating the charges and citing the evidence that supported escape, attempted murder, manslaughter, murder. I set forth my various theories of causation and argued that George Wieber was an unwitting participant in Richardson's escape. Wieber had just left the stand. My argument had been dry on paper, but in the courtroom it came alive. Lastly, I reviewed for the court the history of the felony-murder statute and showed how it evolved.

Justice Warner, interested in what I had to say, questioned me closely as I went along. I began to feel confident. My case would get to the jury.

After I had finished, Kunstler made a few additional remarks; then without further ado, the judge denied his motion.

27

The Defense

It was Kunstler's turn.

With the end of my direct case, the initiative passed to him. He would be the one to call witnesses to the stand, to shape and mold the flow of testimony to suit his ends. He had promised during his voir dire that he would reveal my case as a fraud, and now the time had come for him to deliver.

Throughout the trial, Kunstler had not given a clue to the particulars of his defense. I worried that he might have a bombshell that would radically transform the nature of the trial. For example, did he have a witness, unknown to us, who had been at the Hunts Point station? Would there be other witnesses from Lincoln Hospital to take issue with my presentation? Had he obtained expert witnesses to contradict my medical or ballistics testimony? Would Richardson himself take the stand? I considered all of these possibilities, and worked late getting ready to respond.

Kunstler began the defense of his client outside the hearing of the jury by seeking rulings from Justice Warner on the scope of the evidence that he would be permitted to offer in Richardson's behalf. Just as I had sought an advance ruling on the admissibility of the defendant's arrest warrants at the beginning of my case, Kunstler began by asking permission to introduce evidence about "other police killings in the city, and what happened to the police officers involved." He was particularly interested in the Glover and Reese cases, both of which involved the fatal shooting of young blacks by police officers. His legal justification for offering such evidence was something that he called "selective prosecution." He said, "It's selective prosecution, Judge, that's the idea; as a defense, if they prosecute Richardson and don't prosecute the other guy . . ."

I had been expecting this. Kunstler wanted to convert the Richardson trial into a political seminar on racially motivated police brutality. If permitted, he would have held an open inquest on every police killing of a member of a minority in the history of the city. Such evidence could be relied upon to inflame the passions of a racially balanced jury, and would be sure to distract attention from the narrow factual question of Richardson's guilt or innocence. Indeed, the same logic allowing Kunstler to introduce random evidence of police brutality would also have permitted me to parade before the jury evidence about the murders of other police officers. Such a ruling would have turned the trial into a circus.

I knew that there was no real basis to Kunstler's "selective prosecution" theory, and I strongly opposed it: ". . . to argue selective prosecution [as Mr. Kunstler has] the defense would have to assert that this man (Richardson) was singled out from among a class of people who are identically situated. Now that would require us to sit here and re-try . . . each and every police shooting in the City of New York and then make a factual determination whether somehow [in each case] there was something different that happened . . . It's patently ridiculous.

"This case has to stand or fall on its own merits, as I think anyone who has anything to do with this case knows. This case is unique on its facts . . . Richardson is not being singled out and prosecuted when others similarly situated are not. There is no one who has ever been in a similar situation . . ."

Justice Warner listened, and then ruled that Kunstler would not be permitted to introduce evidence beyond the narrow focus of the indictment.

Kunstler was not through. Before the trial I had turned over to the defense a copy of Skagen's personnel file, and from this Kunstler had learned of the incident that occurred in 1971, when Skagen, off duty, had drawn his service revolver during a dispute with his younger sister's boyfriend. No shot had been fired, no violence had erupted, and no one was hurt. Nevertheless, the incident had been reported, and Skagen had been disciplined by the Police Department.

Kunstler told Justice Warner of his intention of mentioning this incident to the jury. He explained: "He [Mr. Phillips] has said [that Skagen] pulled his gun legitimately; and if there is evidence that at another time he pulled the gun [il] legitimately, [the jury] ought to have that. This is not an ordinary person, Judge . . . and there is a presumption . . . in the public mind [that] when a police officer pulls his gun, he does it for legal purposes . . They are vouching . . . that [Skagen] used it here for legitimate business. If on another occasion he did not, I think the jury is entitled to know that . . ."

The judge questioned Kunstler closely on his motives. Was the purpose of the introduction of this testimony to show that Skagen had violent propensities? Kunstler agreed that this indeed was his purpose, which proved fatal to his argument.

The judge turned to me. "Let me hear from Mr. Phillips."

MR. PHILLIPS: Judge, I have violent objection to the application by Mr. Kunstler. The law . . . is clear [and] persuasive, and I suggest . . . that it is just. That law unqualifiedly says that the character, the propensities, the background, the history of a deceased may not be interjected into a homicide case, except under very, very special circumstances which do not apply in this case. Now . . . let me make a couple of points . . . The first . . . is that [this] incident has no relevance . . . at all to this case. [It] was a family

matter [in which] his sister had been [beaten] . . . by her fiance
. . . Even assuming that . . . he drew the gun wrongfully, it has no
bearing at all, either in logic or inlaw, as to what he would do
on his way home from a day's work upon meeting a total stranger . . .

THE COURT: Are you saying [that] in no event, Mr. Phillips—

MR. PHILLIPS: Only in one event, and that's if Mr. Richardson gets
on the stand and says, "Yes, I know John Skagen is a violent man,
and that's why I reacted the way I did . . ." If he gets on the stand
and says . . . that he was acting in self-defense that day, because
he knew that Skagen was a gun-happy guy . . . then I would
concede . . . that [Mr. Kunstler] would be entitled to bring in the
character of John Skagen.

The law was with me. We went to the books, and it quickly
became apparent that except for a self-defense claim, it is
improper in a homicide trial to introduce evidence on the
violent propensities, if any, of the deceased. Bound by the law,
Judge Warner denied Kunstler's application.

With the jury present, Kunstler again waived his right to
make an opening statement. He was still playing it close to the
vest, giving no clues to the direction the defense would take.

Dr. Taft took the stand again. He was unkempt, with long,
stringy blond hair, wearing workman's clothing and motorcycle
boots. I do not believe that his appearance made a good impression on the jury.

Taft's testimony on direct examination was brief, essentially a replay of his testimony at the hearing. There was one
important exception: this time he did not mention anything
about Richardson's head being bloody, as if he had been
beaten. That testimony had not gone over well at the hearing,
and I was pleased that it did not surface at the trial. Instead,
the burden of Dr. Taft's testimony was that he had reviewed
Richardson's hospital record, and that in his opinion the prisoner was not rational that night while being questioned because the pain and the drugs that had been administered had
clouded his mind.

I enjoyed cross-examining Dr. Taft. I began by attacking

his expertise. I established that not only was he not a surgeon, but that he'd had no training in this field, and that he worked in a drug-detoxification center. After the doctor had conceded that Richardson's problem was a surgical one, I turned to the judge and said, "Your Honor, I object to this man's expertise on the grounds that his testimony is in the surgical area, and . . . by his own admission [he] is involved in a [different] medical field . . ."

My objection was overruled, but I had made my point to the jury. My experts, who were surgeons, were truly knowledge-able about Richardson's physical problems, whereas this wit-ness offered by the defense was out of his depth.

Taft had said that he had seen Richardson on the fateful night, and I asked him for how long a period.

A. . . . I don't think it could have been more that five seconds . . .
Q. At the time that you saw him, where were you?
A. I was standing in . . . the central hallway of the emergency room.
Q. And how far away from him were you . . . ?
A. Approximately twenty feet.
Q. And other than those five seconds, at a distance of twenty feet . . . did you see him at all that evening?
A. No, I didn't.
Q. Did you ever examine him . . . ?
A. No, I didn't.
Q. Did you ever go to his bedside at all?
A. No.

The contrast between my witnesses and Dr. Taft could not have been more glaring. The doctors and the police officers I had put on the stand all had spent a considerable amount of time at the prisoner's bedside, and were testifying about their personal observations rather than making hypothetical pro-nouncements on the possible effects of injuries and drugs on Richardson's mind.

Feeling that he had been thoroughly discredited, I cut short my cross-examination of Dr. Taft.

*   *   *

Cross-examination is easily the most important and difficult skill a trial attorney must master. Its significance is obvious, but few people realize how difficult it is. It requires insight, a great deal of experience, immense poise, a quick wit and a commanding physical presence. Cross-examination was the one area in which my relative inexperience put me at a distinct disadvantage with Kunstler. I simply wasn't in his league when it came to discrediting a hostile witness. He was one of the most technically proficient cross-examiners I had ever seen, and I learned a great deal from him.

What makes cross-examination so difficult is that it must be spontaneous and unrehearsed. Direct examination can be prepared well in advance of trial; witnesses used are generally friendly and can be counted on to make direct examination a cooperative venture. Before such a witness even takes the stand, both he and the attorney should know exactly what questions are going to be asked and exactly what the answers are going to be.

The opposite is true of cross-examination. The witness is almost always hostile, and since the purpose of cross-examination is to discredit him—to make him seem a liar, a fool or an incompetent—you are not likely to win cooperation. As often as not, you have never met the person before, and the testimony that he gives on direct examination will be new to you. A precise, detailed cross-examination cannot be prepared in advance, but has to be improvised on the spur of the moment. You must listen carefully to the direct examination, and then, without any opportunity to reflect upon the testimony, stand up and match wits with the witness. It is an extremely difficult thing to do.

Of course, there are techniques to successful cross-examination, and books have been written on the subject. We are all taught never to ask any open-ended questions on cross-examination. Never give a witness an opportunity to give lengthy, self-serving answers. Questions should be pointed, calling for brief yes or no answers. The objective is to pin the witness down and to highlight the weaknesses, improbabilities and inconsistencies in his testimony. The pitfall to avoid at all costs is to give the witness an opportunity to repeat and reinforce the damaging testimony he has given on direct examination.

Mary Johnson Lowe, now an acting Supreme Court judge but previously one of the best homicide defense attorneys in New York, once told me that the secret to successful cross-examination was to listen not only to what a witness says on direct examination, but also to what he doesn't say. "Listen for the logical gaps in the testimony," she said, "the comments the witness should have made, but didn't. That's where a witness is vulnerable. For instance, if the victim of a nighttime robbery is making an in-court identification of the robber and you don't hear anything on direct examination about the lighting conditions or what the robber was wearing, the chances are good that the lighting was bad and that the witness doesn't remember what the robber was wearing. Then you know where to go after him." It was good advice.

Another thing that I learned about cross-examination was to be brief, make what points I could, and then sit down. Cross-examinations that lead to total recantations occur only on television. In the courtroom the most that can reasonably be hoped for is to cast a little doubt upon the honesty or accuracy of a witness's testimony.

But cross-examination is an art that does not exist in a vacuum; it is also a means toward an end. It must be subordinated to the ultimate goal of obtaining a favorable verdict. A forceful cross-examination that reduces a witness to little more than a pitiable wreck can be a disaster if the jury begins to feel sorry for or to identify with the person on the stand. Nothing is worse than giving a jury the impression that you are bullying or taking unfair advantage of a sympathetic witness. It is a delicate and often perilous business. Knowing when *not* to cross-examine is as important as knowing how to do it well.

Next, Kunstler called seven young men to the stand who were all James Richardson's friends. They had grown up with him, worked with him, "hung out" with him, played basketball with him. As character witnesses, each briefly spoke a few kind words about the defendant. He was a nice guy; they liked him; he was not prone to violence; none of them could believe that he would carry a gun, let alone shoot a cop. Kunstler did not spend more than five minutes with any of them.

I was also brief; I would see no point in attacking them at length. After establishing that they were all partisans who wanted to see their friend acquitted, I asked each of them whether he had actually seen Richardson on the evening of June 28, 1972. No. Did any of them have any personal knowledge about what had actually happened at the Hunts Point subway station that evening? Of course the answers were negative. I looked at the jury; that was enough. They knew the truth about what had happened; they had heard from the people who had been there.

The next defense witness was Dr. David Spain, a pathologist with a truly impressive set of credentials. He was the director of laboratory services in pathology at a large New York hospital, and a clinical professor of pathology at both New York University Medical School and the Columbia University College of Physicians and Surgeons. For many years he had served as a consultant to the Westchester County Medical Examiner's Office, and had written voluminously on the field of pathology. There was no disputing his expertise.

Dr. Spain's testimony was extremely damaging to my case. He acknowledged that he had not personally witnessed the Skagen autopsy, and was basing his testimony entirely upon medical records and reports prepared by other physicians. Nevertheless, he asserted unequivocally that in his opinion

John Skagen's death had been caused by the three .38 caliber bullets fired by George Wieber. He characterized the two shoulder wounds as trivial, and refused to concede that they contributed to Skagen's death in any way. He was openly critical of the work done at the New York medical examiner's office, and did not shrink from describing their efforts as "unprofessional" and incorrect. It was strong testimony, and it directly challenged my contention that the wounds inflicted by Richardson's gun had helped cause John Skagen's death. If Dr. Spain was believed, or even if he cast a reasonable doubt on the subject, the jury might well reject my homicide counts.

At the time, I did not think that my cross-examination of Dr. Spain was successful. I fenced with him verbally for some time but I never could get him to back an inch off the position that he had taken in his direct testimony. He went to great lengths to minimize the seriousness of the two shoulder wounds, even asserting that there had been no bleeding, or a few drops at most, from the shoulder wounds. I could sense his hostility toward me as I cross-examined him, and eventually I decided to give up and get him off the stand before he could do any more damage.

I was concerned about Spain's testimony. It was the first element in the defense so far that had seriously hurt my case.

That afternoon, when court had recessed for the day, Al the Opera Singer approached me. "Mr. Phillips," he said, "that doctor they called today sure was all wet."

"Why?" I asked, surprised and delighted to hear such an opinion.

"Because he said that a guy who's been shot twice in the shoulder ain't gonna bleed. Any idiot knows that if you get shot twice in the shoulder you're gonna bleed plenty. Don't worry, Mr. Phillips, the jury won't believe that guy."

I did worry, but I felt better about Dr. Spain's testimony after my conversation with Al.

After Dr. Spain left the stand, Kunstler rested his case. All of a sudden the testimony was over. After all these weeks, there were to be no more witnesses, no more exhibits, no more cross-examinations. It took a few moments for the thought to sink in.

When it did, I realized that James Richardson was not going to take the stand. The jury would never hear what he had to say for himself. He would never become real to them and his story would remain untold.

From the beginning, the jury had been told that Richardson was not obliged to take the stand, and that no negative inferences should be drawn from his failure to do so. They had been instructed not to speculate about the reasons why he might choose not to testify, and during the voir dire they had all agreed that they would not consider this damaging. But of course this is contrary to human nature; it is truly impossible to completely ignore the failure of a man charged with murder to testify on his own behalf. The thought must occur to a juror that if he were falsely accused of so terrible a crime as murder, he would shout his innocence from the rooftops. Certainly, he would want the jury to hear his side of the story and to see what kind of a man he was. Such thoughts are inevitable. I believe that juries, no matter how much they are instructed to the contrary, hold against a defendant his failure to take the stand. At least some of them are bound to speculate about the reasons for this failure, and such speculations can do a defendant no good.

In another sense, the jurors were bound to resent Richardson's failure to testify: by this decision, he was in effect depriving them of evidence that would have assisted them in making a decision. Juries, especially in murder cases, are well aware of the serious consequences of their verdicts, and certainly this one must have wanted to hear Richardson speak. It would have made it easier for them to arrive at a verdict if they could size him up on the stand. Some jurors looked puzzled when Kunstler rested, as if they could not really believe that his client would not defend himself.

I cannot really know, of course, why the decision was made to keep Richardson off the stand. Certainly, Kunstler was too experienced to ignore the fact that this failure would hurt his case. Perhaps he felt that the effect of the defendant's testimony, followed by what was bound to be a lengthy and vigorous cross-examination, would be even more damaging.

28

Summing Up

We were reaching the end of the road. I was pleased with the way the trial had gone, and had no desire to prolong it with rebuttal testimony. The time had come for the prosecution and the defense to sum up.

Summing up in a criminal trial is a throwback to an earlier age. It is one of the few arts left in which time is of no consequence. Standing before twelve people, a lawyer can be brief or lengthy—the choice is his own; there are no interruptions, and a captive audience. All that matters are those twelve people; they must be persuaded, or everything that has gone before is in vain. Summation is the one place where lawyers *do* make a difference; if an attorney can be said to "win" or "lose" a case, the chances are that he did so in his closing argument to the jury.

The appeal of a summation may be to the heart, the intellect or the belly—or to all of them. There are as many different ways of summing up as there are trial lawyers, and there is no one correct way to deliver a summation, or to learn how to give one. It is largely a matter of instinct and of experience. Either you are able to reach out and move people with your words or you are not, and that is all there is to it.

Summations are wonderful theater, the one medium where the antique art of spellbinding lives on. Where else, in this age of McLuhan, can one observe a man standing on his feet for two or three hours, uninterrupted, holding a rapt audience in his power? I love summations, both listening to and delivering them.

Kunstler began his summation at 10:30 A.M. and spoke until 1 P.M. without a break. His voice was deep and sonorous, his demeanor composed. He was extremely impressive, looking the jurors right in the eye and talking directly to them. It became clear that summation was where he meant to win this case.

Mr. Foreman, ladies and gentlemen, Mr. Phillips, Mr. Richardson, your Honor.

This is what is known as the summation for the defense, and I have to tell you a little bit about it first, because there are some important aspects that you have to help me with. In essence, I will not have the last word in this case. Mr. Phillips will . . . Therefore a lot of what I say may vanish when you're listening to him . . . If the system is to have any fairness, you must struggle to keep in mind some of the things I say, and those of you that think some of the things I say are important must . . . remember them in [the] jury room during deliberations . . .

I am arguing to persuade you that the prosecution has not done what it set out to do. Mr. Phillips will argue that it has. We're both arguing from our own points of view. The law is a persuasive profession—lawyers are persuaders—yet we have to make sense as well.

So in listening to me you have to consider whether . . . I'm making sense . . . Try to recall and keep it fresh when you hear Mr. Phillips' summation, because he will paint a very dark picture of this defendant. He'll tell you he deceived the police officers, that he should be convicted of murder in the first degree, that he's dangerous and a number of other things which I'm sure you can anticipate in listening to him. I . . . hope that you will not be stampeded, and I'm sure that you will not let . . . your rational[ity] run away. There is emotionalism in this case. A man died, and how can anybody be unemotional about [that]?

And yet I am asking you not . . . to convict a man about whom you have a reasonable doubt. I am hoping you will not let any [motive such as allaying] crime in the City or any of those other endless questions that we asked at the beginning of the voir dire [sway you] . . . [I am] hoping that you will remember those questions and your answers, and that long, dreary jury-selection process, which has as its purpose bringing us to this moment . . . If any of your feelings about what you answered was different than . . . you stated, then, of course . . . the whole process would be meaningless . . .

You have had a chance to watch James Richardson, to watch me, to watch Mr. Phillips . . . You've heard many things, seen many things . . . You all know it's an intricate, involved, even bizarre case, [and] therefore . . . a difficult case for a jury . . . It's filled with all sorts of complexities and . . . tragedy . . . with testimony that is sometimes conflicting . . . it's filled with the stuff of life itself.

Now, I just have a few words before I go into the essential evidence to discuss with you. What I'm going to try to do is to . . . refer to the transcripts and to the evidence. I'm going to replay some of that evidence for you by reading some of the testimony before you, and . . . to try to indicate how the pieces fall or do not fall into place . . . You will recall [that] in the beginning I made some statements to you about the fact that there might be fabrications in this case, statements which I'm prepared to live up to and to discuss with you. I made statements about self-defense . . . in the voir dire questions, and I'm going to try to live up to everything that I said . . .

After I have finished, the defense . . . [has] nothing further [to] do . . . Mr. Phillips will take over . . . [He] is a capable attorney. He will probably tell you that he hasn't had my years of experience, and he may even say that he doesn't have my eloquence or power of persuasion. That is a tactic that is always used; don't be persuaded by it. Mr. Phillips is a capable lawyer . . . as capable as I am . . . He's also as eloquent as I am and . . . is at no disadvantage whatsoever . . . we are all equal before you . . .

Kunstler changed gears quickly, though, and began to take me to task. I had misled the jury, and they could not rely upon my word. Inevitably, some of the details of my long opening statement had not been developed in the ebb and flow of testimony over the weeks. Every important detail that I promised to deliver had been explored, but some minor ones had not. Kunstler seized upon these, recounting them at length and insinuating that I was attempting to mislead the jury. He devoted a great deal of effort to discrediting me. In a way, I should have been flattered. I was being paid a backhanded compliment by this attack, for it suggested that Kunstler was concerned with the impact I had made. But I was not flattered; it made me angry to hear him insinuate that I was being dishonest, and I began to steam.

Eventually Kunstler began to develop the major motif of his summation. For him the case was a conspiracy, though only a little one:

. . . Jacobsen and Wieber are involved in a situation in which . . . one of them kills a police officer . . . The fabrication is not a monumental [one] . . . where the commissioner sits down with the district attorney and they . . . work out how [to] pin that murder on Richardson . . . [It] . . . didn't occur like that . . . Wieber knew he had grievously wounded a police officer when Richardson was still at the fence because he came over, you remember, and said to Jacobsen, "I think I shot a cop." So he knew right away. From that point on the die was cast . . . There had to be someone, and there was a convenient someone . . . We are not fools. They had a convenient person. Maybe it was a fight with Skagen? I don't know. I don't know what happened in this case, but . . . if you charge him with murder and say he deceived everybody . . . then . . . Wieber and the police have no problems.

Now Kunstler lashed at the police. They were lying, covering up, trying to protect their careers, and were quite ready to convict an innocent man to do so. Kunstler was a true believer preaching the gospel in the Bible Belt. He knew who the devil was, and it was his intention to exorcise him.

They call that [41st] precinct Fort Apache because they say it's
. . . like a Wild West fort. This might indicate how they view the
people who live around their precinct . . . [It] creates an attitude on
their parts. They are holding the west against the Indians; they are
holding civilization intact in Fort Apache in the Bronx . . . Having
just come from the Wounded Knee trial . . .
MR. PHILLIPS: Your Honor, I object . . .
MR. KUNSTLER: Withdrawn.

Kunstler seemed inexhaustible. As he went on and on, you
could hear a pin drop in the courtroom.

. . . Mr. Richardson has a family. We did not put them on. We
did put on people who are friends of his because where do you get
character witnesses from—enemies?
. . . Mr. Phillips would ask his inevitable question, "You're a good
friend of the defendant? You want to see him win?"
The implication of that question is "You're all a bunch of liars.
You're doing this solely because you want him to win." Of course
they want him to win, but does that automatically mean that they
. . . perjure themselves?
There's a motive for lying . . . just as there's a motive for all those
police officers . . . But the motive here . . . I think you have to take
into consideration as being somewhat different from the motive of
police officers . . . They told you a little bit about him . . . and they
told you some more things that aren't so apparent. They told you how
the hospital staff put up nickels and dimes, put up the bond for him,
after he spent a year and a half in jail . . . He's still working at the
hospital . . . every day . . . If the Court breaks by four, he goes and
works a full day. That's the kind of man he is.
Even when he found Elaine William's material and returned it
to her . . . that's an indication. Maybe he kept the badge . . . [but]
he never used it if he kept it . . . Somebody rifled her bag in a bar
and . . . threw . . . away the stuff that means nothing to a thief, but
means everything to you . . . nurse's license, a driver's license, her
social security, et cetera. What kind of a man is it that finds that and
sends her a telegram . . . is that a man who murders police officers
of the City of New York . . .? And she wanted to give him money.

He didn't ask for anything . . . She said "At least let me give you a drink." That's a little indication, you know. How many people sitting in this jury box have ever done this when they found anything? I know I've had the opportunity and haven't done it. It is just a pain of the neck . . . to spend $2 for a telegram to someone you don't know . . .

Now, there isn't much more really to say in this case. I have gone through most of my notes and I've pointed out so many things to you that I guess you won't even remember them all . . . I'm asking you to mull over some of the things I've said and see if they make sense to you.

[James Richardson is] charged with the most serious crime known in law: murder. I'm asking you not to compromise on him, not to say, "Well, I don't think he's guilty of anything, but we'll split the apple between us" . . . I'm asking you . . . to not make this a bargaining game between you. It is too serious.

Here's a man who has been in jail a year, has been seriously wounded [and] spent time in the hospital . . . He's now back working again in the hospital. I'm asking you not to compromise . . . this is not [like] settling an insurance claim.

I'm asking those of you who think he is not guilty . . . that you hold firm . . . better a hung jury than a miscarriage of justice . . . There is too much at stake here for anything quick or precipitous. Or anything that may make you some day wake up screaming in the middle of the night and wonder, "My God, what have I done?"

I'm asking you to consider everything that you told us when you were sworn here as jurors: your assurances . . . that you would not prejudge; that you would seriously consider the evidence . . . and . . . do it fairly and squarely [so] that you would go home and look yourself in the mirror for the rest of your life. That's how serious all of this is.

If you feel that the prosecution has failed . . . after listening to everything, stick to that; it is not the purpose of the law to bargain away when you don't believe [in order] to . . . get it over with . . This is one of the most important moments . . . that . . . you and I will have. I say this in many cases because they are all important. They . . . all [involve] human lives in one way or another which have for a moment been entrusted to . . . us and which we dispose of . . . I'm asking you in making that disposition to be absolutely certain before you do so.

I will end as I began because in the beginning I went through some of the things that Mr. Phillips had said and because, as you must know . . . I think there is something wrong with this case. I . . . think something evil or bad or incompetent or negligent occurred . . . Think about it and I think you will see this business corrupts . . . everyone who touches it . . . It's very simple. All you want to do is clear an officer and prevent him from being hurt . . . and pin it on someone that is in some way involved.

We don't know what really happened down there, but James Richardson, we will assume for the sake of argument, is in some way involved. Something happened; I don't know what it was. You have to ask yourselves whether in the light of everything and thinking of the arguments I have made, have they proved him guilty beyond a reasonable doubt . . . ? Analyze it closely, because the decision you make may well be irrevocable . . . particularly in [a case as] intricate as this one . . . It has to be essentially the most serious decision you make in your life—the same decision you would want twelve others to make for you if you were sitting where James Richardson is sitting. Not a very pleasant place to sit, I can assure you.

I want to thank you all for listening . . . I thought that there was a great deal of attention paid . . . I watched you . . . through all the witnesses, and I know you will—I hope you will—do right in this case because the implications are enormous. Our system is beset on all sides by critics, some more strident than others, and I must say I am one of the most strident . . . If it is workable . . . it would . . . be . . . because of juries like yourself, who all across this land have learned to tell what is right and what is wrong and when the government is lying and when it is not. Thank you all very much."

THE COURT: Ladies and gentlemen of the jury, at this time we will recess for lunch. Return at 2:15 promptly. In the interim you are not to discuss this case or any aspects of it, either among yourself or with anyone else. You are not to let anyone discuss it with you or interfere with you in any way. Should anyone attempt to discuss this case or interfere with you in any way I expect you to report that fact to me . . .

The defense had had the morning; the prosecution would have the afternoon. I should have been worried. Kunstler had painted a dark picture of the prosecution, one of deceit and conspiracy, and he had been persuasive. It was a picture that might well appeal to certain jurors. I had my job cut out for me. Oddly, I was not concerned. I was well prepared, and I knew with a certainty that I cannot explain that I would deliver a far better summation than Kunstler had. I had come to believe strongly that Richardson was guilty, and that what I had to say to the jury would be the truth of what had happened. I was certain that they would believe me.

The one emotion that I did feel after Kunstler's summation was anger. I was angry that he'd had accused me of trying to deceive a jury. His remarks had been personal, and I took them personally. The lunch break was spent harnessing that anger and putting it to work.

From the minute my summation began that afternoon I felt good. I was at home in front of this jury, and felt in harmony with them. I thanked them for their attention and then got down to business. For only the second time in the trial, I raised my voice and let my anger show:

He [Kunstler] said that basically two things happened here, and that's why you must have a reasonable doubt. He said first there is a diabolically evil plot here—a frame-up, I think . . . was the term he used. And he accused me. He said that I deceived you . . . which is a polite way of saying that I was a liar. First he said that this case is a . . . diabolically conceived plot . . . but then he says . . . that [it] is sloppy . . . [that] there are so many contradictions throughout this case that you have to . . . realize that it could not have possibly happened the way the prosecution said it happened.

Now we can't have it both ways. Either it is a diabolical . . . plot by extremely brilliant and evil people . . . or else it's . . . sloppy and improbable. But he has to have it both ways, because in fact it's neither way. What you heard from the witnesses was an uncontradicted and truthful story, uncontradicted by any evidence or testimony to the contrary as to the defendant's guilt.

Kunstler had made his summation personal, and I was replying in kind. I had to set the tone of my summation. The jury must be made to see from the outset the inherent weakness of the defense's conspiracy–self-defense argument. On the one hand, Kunstler was portraying Richardson as an innocent framed for doing nothing; on the other, he was picking at details, tacitly acknowledging that Richardson had been involved but asserting that it had not happened exactly the way the prosecution had portrayed it. His argument had been inconsistent, shuttling back and forth between two irreconcilable lines of defense. I hammered away at this, emphasizing over and over Kunstler's inability to seize upon a single persuasive line of defense.

Then the time came to get down to brass tacks. I lowered my voice, and was pleased to see the jury lean forward expectantly. I was in command.

Now, I am going to go through the charges that are leveled against Mr. Richardson . . . one by one, and as I go through them I am going to ask you to think to yourselves, "Is there enough evidence on this charge to convict this man?" . . . I'm going to go through these charges starting from the end of the indictment and going [back] to the beginning of the indictment, and as I go along you will see why . . . Let's get down to the specific evidence, because . . . you have to decide whether the evidence is there to convict this man of [one] crime or of seven crimes.

. . . You are here to decide whether or not James Richardson had a gun; whether he had a stolen shield and knew it was stolen; whether or not he escaped. That's what you have to decide. All the rest of the details are on the periphery. Let's go to the heart of the matter and . . . let's then decide whether or not he's guilty of the crimes charged . . . We will start with the last charge . . . the possession of stolen property . . . I was astounded during the defendant's summation because Mr. Kunstler . . . told you that the man was guilty of having a stolen shield . . . Did you hear him say something like that? I think I did. It's your memory that counts. He was practically telling you that on June 28, 1972 . . . James Richardson, this paragon of virtue in the community, had a stolen officer's badge on him.

Do you think he had the stolen officer's badge because he wanted to teach the kids in the community how to grow up straight and be good citizens? Mr. Kunstler said he didn't know why James Richardson had the badge. Why do *you* think he had the badge . . . ? And, by the way, do you have any doubt in your mind that he knew it was stolen? You heard Mrs. Williams. Mr. Kunstler said nothing about her credibility because he accepted it. Do you doubt for a minute [that] she asked where her badge was? Of course she did. She said she did, and [that Richardson] said, "I never found it. I never had it." And lo and behold, it shows up in the subway station with Mr. Richardson's identification papers . . .

I went on, detailing the evidence supporting each charge, taking the jury step by step through the evidence, and demonstrating how I had delivered on my promise to prove each count of the indictment. Looking the jurors in the eye, I could see their understanding and agreement. I kept returning to the same refrain: Could all of this uncontradicted evidence from civilians, police officers, laymen and experts be deceit and fabrication? Or was it the painful but unadorned truth?

I discussed Sylvester Farish's testimony:

Now if this was a big frame-up, it would not be beyond the power of the police . . . to find someone like Farish to come in and lie and say I saw a gun, and saw the bullets coming out of the gun. But as Mr. Kunstler told you, Farish was telling the truth. Farish was a truthful man in all respects . . . He didn't add anything that he didn't see. What he saw was the man going for his belt and turn[ing] around, and then he heard shots . . . Use your common sense: based upon everything else . . . do you have any doubt in your mind . . that that man [pointing to Richardson] had a gun and was turning around?

I had worked up a full head of steam, and with each minute my impact upon the jury was becoming more powerful. I had them in my sway. Finally, Kunstler decided to break up the flow of my rhetoric, and as I was discussing the youths and the recovery of the .32 caliber Clerke in the railroad yard, he objected:

MR. KUNSTLER: Your Honor, that is a gross misstatement to this jury.
THE COURT: Just a moment.
MR. KUNSTLER: There was no testimony—
MR. PHILLIPS: Your Honor—
THE COURT: Just a moment. Members of the jury; it is your recollection of the testimony in this case that will control, not what either counsel says. It's your recollection of the testimony. Proceed, please.
MR. PHILLIPS: [As] I said from the beginning, I'm going to tell you my recollection . . . Kunstler stood up in front of you for three hours and talked about a million things, and I held my peace because you have a right to hear what he [says]. By the same token, I've got the right to tell you what I honestly believe . . . Listen to what I say and see if it's accurate . . . Listen to what he said and see if it's accurate . . .

I was in no mood to be interrupted by Kunstler and I let this show, appealing to the jury's sense of fairness. Kunstler had had his turn; now I should have mine. Of course he would not agree with the facts as I described them—if he did, there would have been no trial—but it was not right for him to interrupt.

I turned my attention to John Skagen, and asked the jury to reflect upon what had happened between him and Richardson that afternoon:

You know that John Skagen was . . . on his way home; and . . . that he had asked to be excused from . . . night duty because he [had done] day duty. Now, I ask you . . . if you are on your way home from a night's work, even if you're a cop, do you go looking for trouble or are you looking to go home and eat supper? . . . It's five in the afternoon . . . He's not on duty. So . . . why . . . in the world does that man place James Richardson under arrest?

Now, John Skagen is dead . . . so [he] cannot tell you why he did it, but what do we know?

We know [that a] man on his way home is only going to start

acting if he sees something that's a clear and present danger to himself and everybody else . . . [in] that subway. It is pretty clear . . . that Skagen would act only if he saw that one thing that in the mind of [a] cop or any other person signals danger. And what's that thing? It's a gun, it's a Saturday-night special packed in a man's belt. He saw it. That's why they had words . . . Who knows what they said, but . . . it doesn't take too much intelligence to speculate what those . . words are.

Then I focused the jury's attention on Richardson. He was a mystery to them, a physical presence about whom much had been said, but about whom little was really known. Relying upon his character witnesses, Kunstler had attempted to portray him favorably. I presented the other side of the picture:

Now I've already . . . discussed with you the question of escape, and I think that you can see that there is no question that the . . . foremost thing in James Richardson's mind was getting the hell away. He wanted to get out of that subway more badly, probably, than you've wanted to do anything in your life, and, everything that he did from the beginning to the end of this incident was designed to accomplish . . . one thing only . . . to escape. And I submit to you that John Skagen['s] death was caused by . . . Richardson's unholy . . . and unlawful . . . intention of escaping.

And I submit to you . . . that all five of those bullets [in Skagen's body were] a direct consequence of Richardson's desire to escape, and that he put two bullets through the man's shoulder by his own direct action, and . . . he . . . set up those other three.

Now what do I mean by "set up those other three"? . . . I'm going to return to Richardson's own evidence as presented. You heard Richardson's friends . . . tell about what a fine fellow he was, and . . that Richardson is a cool head, Richardson's a man for a crisis when the going gets rough . . . It would seem that Richardson spent his entire boyhood playing basketball, learning to react fast. We can now couple that with what happened in the station.

Richardson's in a jam, he's got a big problem, he's up against the wall and he's got to think fast. But we know that [he] is a man who can think fast and . . . react fast, so he figures . . . not me, I'm not going to jail, I'd rather escape, I'd rather take my chances . . .

He turns and fires those shots. So far, so good . . . [The] cop could have shot him right then and there, but he got away with that . . . Then he's running up the stairs and he knows Skagen's chasing him . . . and . . . he's got to get away fast . . . and what does he see? He sees . . . two uniformed cops, no question about it . . .

Some men . . . might have given up. Not Richardson, the cool head . . . the guy you want on your side. He sees the cops in that split second it takes . . . for a man in a tight situation . . . so he shouts, "There's a crazy man shooting, there's a crazy man shooting."

He knows what's going to happen next. Not that they are going to kill Skagen, mind you; he doesn't have to intend that, and the Judge will charge you . . . that . . . his . . . only purpose . . . was to get the hell out of there. Oh, he was ready to kill down here to escape, no question about it, [but] by the time he is running up the stairs all of that's gone; he just wants . . . to get out. . . . It almost worked—in fact, it did work, except that he didn't get away. But his hope was merely . . . that the uniformed cops and the off-duty cops would tangle . . . with one another, and while they were straightening it out —good bye Richardson.

That's what he had in mind . . . and it worked with Wieber . . . [but not] Jacobsen . . .

A few minutes later, as I was talking about the conflict in testimony between the two medical examiners, Kunstler interrupted again. As my summation kept building in strength, he chose to interject his comments frequently, always trying to call into question my accuracy. This interchange took place while I was making the point that Al the Opera Singer had suggested to me:

Now Dr. Spain said something that was ridiculous . . . [that] the two bullets in the shoulder didn't cause any bleeding. How in the world do you get shot in one side and out the other and not bleed?"
MR. KUNSTLER: Your Honor, he never said a word of that.
MR. PHILLIPS: Your Honor, I submit these interjections are improper.

MR. KUNSTLER: He's telling an untruth, your Honor.

MR. PHILLIPS: Mr. Kunstler told many untruths.

THE COURT: Now just a moment, just a moment. I expect both of you gentlemen to continue [in] the professional manner in which you have conducted yourselves during the last three weeks. Don't expect this afternoon to be any different than all of the others. All right, let's proceed.

By this point Kunstler and I were snarling at each another; there was no pretense at civility and no vestige of good will left.

My summation was building to a climax, and at last I addressed myself to the question of police shootings. I had thought long and hard about this question from the very beginning. I knew that what I was about to say would hurt Pat Skagen terribly, and I was very much aware of her presence, but it had to be said. I lowered my voice almost to a whisper. The jury was still under my control.

Some of this is going to be a little painful . . . a little bit ugly, but it's true, I submit.

You [have] heard the term "trigger-happy" [and] some very emotional language [from Mr. Kunstler] about police officers firing guns. We've spent . . . a full month going over, again and again . . . the question of whether or not the four cops . . . should have fired their guns. Do you realize that we're here . . . to decide something the cops had one second to make up their minds about—one second during which their lives were on the line . . . Men were pointing guns at them . . . and they had to decide like this [snapping fingers] . . . Just remember that when you assess their testimony . . . Three cops . . . saw the situation, sized it up and shot immediately, and they came into court to tell you about it. They are alive today and they . . . told you about it. And there's a fourth cop . . . John Skagen, and he stood there with a gun at Richardson's back and he hesitated and he's dead because he hesitated. So when you speculate . . . about what cops ought to do . . . remember the difference between Skagen, who is dead, and the other three, who are alive . . .

. . . George Wieber . . . sees that man with a gun out and he's heard shots. He doesn't say, "Who are you?" because while you're saying [that] you can have four bullets put into your body. He shoots; he assesses the situation as best he can under terrible conditions and he does the best he can.

. . . Mr. Kunstler used a very apt phrase . . . He said George Wieber is a tragic figure. I submit to you that he's right . . . Tragedy is an interesting concept if you think about . . . what it really means. A tragic figure is a [person] who comes to grief not because he's a bum [nor] because he's inept, but . . . because he's excellent. George Wieber did exactly what he was trained to do and he did it well, and he's an excellent cop . . . The only man who did not do exactly what he should have done was John Skagen . . . That's a tragedy, and John Skagen is dead, so he has paid the last full price . . .

. . . The villain of this case is James Richardson . . . who set the ball in motion . . . that led George Wieber . . . into a situation [for which he will suffer] all the rest of his life . . . If you have any doubts . . . just remember George Wieber . . . on the stand. Did you see the torture on that man's face? . . . Do you remember that?

I had spoken some hard words, and was eager to move on. At the heart of the case there was an ugly truth about Skagen, Richardson and Wieber—a truth about survival and the will to live. I had touched upon that truth gingerly, and was glad to leave it behind me. Returning to the familiar frame-up theme, I took Kunstler to task once again:

You may recall [that Mr. Kunstler began] by saying, "I'm not saying that the Police Commission, Mayor Lindsay and the D.A.'s office are part of the frame-up. It is just a little frame-up dreamed up by the one or two cops."

But then as he goes along . . . he says, "Well, Wieber was certainly part of the frame-up." Then he adds Jacobsen . . . the ballistics man . . . The D.A. has been misleading you [so] you might infer he's part of the frame-up. The police technicians—you can't really trust them because they're policemen, so they're part of the frame-up too. The medical examiner works for the City, so he's not being honest with you either . . . So before he's done this little frame-up . . . has turned into a big frame-up . . .

Either there is a frame-up or there isn't . . . If you're going to frame a man, then you frame him so it sticks. The first question you've got to ask [is], if it is a frame-up, why is [Richardson] here at all, why didn't he die that day? . . . If the evil police were looking to get this guy, . . . there [need] not even have been a trial . . . I submit to you it is ridiculous . . . Why the contradictions?

. . . Now, ladies and gentlemen, I'll be sitting down in just a moment . . . I want to conclude again by thanking you for your attention. I know it's been very difficult. This has been a long day for you. You swore an oath, each of you, as a juror [that] . . . you would be fair and impartial and . . . would make your decision on the facts as you heard them . . . I ask you to uphold that oath . . . I don't think there is anybody that envies you this duty . . . I ask you to vote your conscience, and I expect you to . . . Realize that there are times that life forces all of us to face up to unpleasant acts and to do something that we might not wish to do . . . You have sworn an oath to do this difficult job, and I expect you to do no less. I expect you to all talk calmly and rationally with one another, as you promised you would, and I expect you all to . . . to reach accord.

. . . I thank you very much.

29

Charge and Verdict

When I sat down after my summation, I was drained. My throat was parched, but though light-headed i felt good. I didn't need to be told I had done well; I knew I had. For the first time since the trial began, I was able to savor a feeling of confidence. I was going to win.

I looked across the courtroom at Kunstler. He was glaring at me. The reserves of good will that I had carefully cultivated throughout the trial had dissipated. We had just publicly spoken harshly of each other, and whatever common sympathies or beliefs that might have bound us together under other circumstances were forgotten. We had been cast in adversarial roles, and in fulfilling these roles we had become enemies, at least for a time. Later I would come to regret this; at the time I did not care.

I expected that now we would go home for the night. Six hours of impassioned oratory struck me as enough for one day. Everyone seemed exhausted, and it would have been better to start fresh the next morning with the judge's charge and the jury's deliberations.

Justice Warner did not agree. To my surprise, he did not adjourn the trial. Instead, after a ten-minute recess, he launched right into his charge to the jury, and for two hours lectured the panel on the law of the case.

A judge's charge to a jury is an amazing exercise in optimism. For two or three hours he reads to twelve laymen enough law to keep a law student busy for a semester. Twelve individuals, selected more or less at random, sit there, unable to take notes or ask questions. Somehow, just by listening, it is presumed that everything spoken by the judge will take root in their collective intelligence.

In practice it is unrealistic to expect total comprehension. There is just too much law dispensed too quickly, and it is unfair to expect jurors to become jurists. But this is not the point. We have long rejected the system, common in some European countries, of having judges participate with lay jurors in their deliberations. Here we place a greater trust in the intellectual and moral capacities of our citizens, and in their ordinary common sense. It is a trust that is not misplaced. Anyone who has had the privilege of sitting through a number of jury trials cannot help but be impressed by the fairness and wisdom of the average American jury. They are in deadly earnest, deeply aware of the gravity of their function, and I am convinced that they both understand and honor the law in its essentials during deliberation. You would have to search hard to find a practicing trial lawyer who felt differently.

Justice Warner had the last word with the jury. With our summations completed, both Kunstler and I were silenced. Only the judge could speak; after the basically passive role of the referee that he had assumed throughout the trial, the time had at last come for Justice Warner to take center stage. He did so with firmness and grace. There was no misunderstanding his words, and no ignoring his earnestness.

He began by warning the jury that the indictment against James Richardson was not proof of guilt but merely an accusation. After he had read them the entire indictment, they were instructed that the presumption of innocence could only be overcome by proof beyond a reasonable doubt to the contrary. Further, they were not to assume that the court had any opinion on the defendant's guilt or innocence; that was solely their province. Then the judge defined reasonable doubt:

A reasonable doubt is a doubt based upon reason . . . a doubt for which the juror . . . can give a reason . . . if called upon to do so. [It] . . . is not a mere . . . surmise that the accused may not be guilty [nor] . . . a doubt based upon sympathy, or the reluctance of a juror to perform a disagreeable task . . .

If you are satisfied to a moral certainty that this defendant . . . is guilty of any one of the crimes charged here, you may safely say that you have been convinced beyond a reasonable doubt. If your mind is wavering, or if you are uncertain . . . you have not been convinced beyond a reasonable doubt and must render a verdict of not guilty . . .

The People are not required to prove the guilt of the defendant beyond *all* doubt. The question of punishment, members of the jury, is one for the Court. You have no right to . . . discuss . . . or speculate about punishment in any way. . . . Your working function is to determine . . . the guilt or innocence of the defendant. Punishment is the duty of the Court . . .

Justice Warner went on to give the jury guidelines for assessing the credibility of witnesses, and said a few words about the special standards applicable to expert witnesses. He also told the jury that they had a right to reject the confessions entirely if they did not believe them to have been voluntarily obtained. Then, count by count, he defined for the jury the law underlying each charge of the indictment. In discussing the homicide counts, he did not mention my elaborate theory of vicarious responsibility for George Wieber's bullets; instead, he stayed with the conventional direct-causation doctrine. This judicial rejection of my legal arguments distressed me; I had hoped to see the theory preserved for appellate review, so that new law might be made on appeal in the event of a conviction.

Since any conviction obtained is presumed to be in accord with the law as charged to the jury, Justice Warner's refusal to mention my theory removed it from the case.

After completing his discussion of the seven counts, Justice Warner turned to other matters:

Under no circumstances are you to report or advise the court on any of your deliberations in the jury room or as to how the jury voted on a particular ballot.

In making the factual determination on which your verdict will be based, you may consider only the testimony of the witnesses as you have heard in this courtroom and the exhibits received into evidence.

Comments, remarks and summation by opposing attorneys are not evidence, nor is anything that I have said with regard to the facts or the evidence.

You are expected to come to an agreement which speaks the truth. Your discussions should be dignified, unimpassioned and intelligent, and based upon the evidence and the law—the evidence as you have understood it and the law as I have given it to you. No juror has a right to affect an arbitrary stand and refuse to discuss the evidence or to close his mind in judgment to the reasons advanced by his fellow jurors. You should always be open to reason, but a juror has a right . . . to stand by his opinion. He should, however, make every effort to blend his judgment with theirs insofar as it can be done with justice . . .

. . . You must not permit your judgment to be beclouded, warped or obscured by passion, feelings, bias or prejudice of any kind. The law of the State of New York has placed in your hands . . . the exclusive right to determine the innocence or guilt of the defendant on trial. The protection of our institutions and our citizens demand that your task be truly rendered. Your verdict should reflect the operation of your minds and not of your hearts. You must not permit yourselves to be diverted from a careful consideration of the evidence in this case, or the rendition of a fair and impartial verdict, by any feelings of sympathy for the defendant, or [be] influenced by any antipathy against the defendant, or [be] swayed by . . prejudice against anyone in this case.

It has been said that the law must be based on justice or else it cannot stand, and it must be enforced with courage and resolute firmness. If you believe this defendant to be guilty beyond a reasonable doubt of the crime or crimes charged, you must not hesitate in the performance of your duty . . . If, on the other hand, you entertain a reasonable doubt of the guilt of the defendant of the crime or crimes charged, your verdict must be not guilty.

You of course realize the importance of this case to the defendant. He must be accorded every right to which he's entitled to under the law . . . and the benefit of every reasonable doubt. On the other hand, the case is important to the People of this State because the security and safety of human lives and the peace and good order of the community depends upon the impartial interpretation of the criminal laws. Give to this defendant every right to which he's entitled, and at the same time give to the People of this State that protection which the proper and impartial interpretation of the law will secure for them.

Please bear in mind, members of the jury, that in a criminal case a verdict is not reached until all twelve jurors have unanimously agreed upon a verdict . . .

I shall now enumerate for you the possible verdicts you may reach:

With respect to count one, Felony Murder, guilty or not guilty;

Count two, Manslaughter in the Second Degree, guilty or not guilty;

Count three, Attempted Murder, guilty or not guilty;

Count four, Escape in the Second Degree, guilty or not guilty;

Count five, Possessing a Weapon as a Felony, guilty or not guilty;

Count six, Reckless Endangerment in the Second Degree, guilty or not guilty;

Count seven, Criminal Possession of Stolen Property in the Third Degree, guilty or not guilty.

Then, abruptly, it was all over. It was seven-thirty in the evening, and we had been at it for nine hours. Justice Warner advised the jury that they would be sequestered during their deliberations, and then he sent them out to eat dinner under the guard of court officers. Afterwards they would start their deliberations. The wait had begun.

I went downstairs to receive the congratulations of Dom Cuccio, Bob Maguire, Richie Gest and the other detectives. Pat Skagen was there. I apologized for the hard things I had been obliged to say about her husband. She indicated that she understood, but I still felt bad about it. The moment passed, and we began to speculate about the verdict. We were all optimistic; the trial, and especially the summations, had gone far better than any of us had anticipated. The judge's charge had been solid and fair, the jury had seemed attentive and well-disposed toward my arguments, and all together the prospects appeared good.

I told Pat and the detectives not to expect a verdict that night. "It's too late. They won't have enough time. Besides, a very rapid verdict is usually an acquittal. Juries take their own sweet time before they send a guy away for murder. We won't get a verdict on this case until tomorrow afternoon or tomorrow evening at the earliest." On that note we all went out to dinner.

When we returned from the restaurant a surprise awaited us. The jury had sent a note down, and Morris Krohn had called from the courtroom requesting my presence there. We all hurried upstairs with only one thing on our minds: Could there be a verdict already?

A few minutes after I arrived, Justice Warner emerged from the robing room with the jury's note. Calling Kunstler and me forward, he showed it to us. It read: "Like to hear the testimony of Mrs. Betancourt, Mr. Sylvester Farish, Newsstand Boy, Mr. C. Klinger. P.S. Legal definition of what constitutes an arrest."

The fact that the jury wanted the testimony of the subway station civilians read back seemed to me a good sign. Perhaps they were following my advice and focusing on the initial confrontation between Skagen and Richardson rather than on the later event out on the street. Still, no one could really know what was on their collective mind. Later, back in my office, we speculated endlessly on the significance of the note, but it was like trying to decipher the meaning of an oracle.

When Justice Warner called the jurors down they looked as if they had been working; some of the men had loosened their ties and were in shirt-sleeves. They took their seats and looked up at the judge expectantly.

We sat for an hour while the court reporter read back the testimony. Then, after Justice Warner read them a brief definition of the word "arrest," the jury filed back upstairs to continue their deliberations. Watching them leave, I wondered whether the testimony and instructions they had just heard would make any difference to them.

Pat Skagen, the detectives and I returned to my office, which was deserted and eerie this late at night. Only the policeman guarding the entire district attorney's office was there. One of the detectives went out for a six pack of beer, but as we sat drinking and telling jokes the tension never really left us. I was exhausted.

At 11:30 P.M. we were summoned back to the courtroom. Justice Warner brought the jury down, told them that he was sending them to a hotel for the night, and that they were to cease deliberations until the following morning.

We all went home except for the jurors, who were locked in their rooms under armed guard. It had been a long day. The next one would be even longer.

I did not sleep very much that night.

The following morning I carefully put on the same suit I had worn the day before—a superstition that some trial lawyers have. The logic behind it is that since the jurors do not have a chance to go home and change their clothing, they may resent seeing a lawyer freshly dressed, but it's really only a superstition that is supposed to bring good luck.

Back in my office that morning we maintained our vigil. Pat Skagen was chain-smoking. All around us, the district attorney's office was following its workaday routine while we sat trying to maintain small talk. Finally I went up to the courtroom. Kunstler was there with a woman assistant. She was knitting and he was doing *The New York Times* crossword puzzle. He looked tired. We didn't speak.

James Richardson was in the hallway outside the courtroom with a few friends. As always, he was expressionless, never giving a clue to what was going on inside.

I said hello to Morris Krohn, then picked up the minutes of the summation and the judge's charge from the court reporter before returning to my office. It was still too early to expect a verdict.

Time dragged on. We ate lunch. Every now and then one of my colleagues would stop by to learn whether a verdict had been reached. Pat Skagen went out to buy more cigarettes.

At 3 P.M. the jury finally sent down another note, and we raced upstairs. They had been deliberating for almost ten hours; surely that was enough time for them to reach a verdict.

When Justice Warner appeared, Kunstler and I read the jury's second note: "Please read Charge #4, Escape Second Degree as in the charge to the jury. Please send up the notes taken by Detective Cruz as placed in evidence. *First* interview James Richardson gave in hospital."

I liked the tenor of this message. If, after all these hours, they were still debating the escape question, then the felony-murder charge on which it was predicated was still a live issue. I felt good.

It was the first time we had seen the jury that day, and we searched their faces for clues. They looked grim, and none of them glanced at James Richardson—a good sign. All the men were in shirt-sleeves now, a bit grizzled and beginning to need fresh clothing.

After Justice Warner gave them Detective Cruz's note and reread his charge on Escape in the Second Degree, the jury returned upstairs and our vigil continued.

The next summons to return to the courtroom came at 5:50 P.M. Again the adrenaline began to flow. At the start of the deliberations, I had bravely predicted a murder conviction around dinner time of the second day. Had I hit the nail on the head?

But it was another note which read: "Please read count one, Felony Murder, as per charge to jury."

Justice Warner announced that he was going to send the jurors out to dinner and instruct them on their return. Though the jurors indicated that they wished to continue deliberating, the judge demurred, and they went out to eat.

Over dinner we talked about the most recent request. I felt that the panel was obviously close to a decision on the murder count, and that there must be a large majority in favor of it. I could not imagine a holdout for conviction with a majority for acquittal; it just wouldn't happen that way. The jury had not looked deadlocked when the judge sent it out to dinner, and I told Pat Skagen that our best hope was a verdict before the evening was over. If they were sent back to their hotel for the night, we could be in trouble. They might bog down, deadlock or worse. Everyone seemed to agree with my assessment. I don't think that any of us tasted our dinner.

When we returned to the courtroom, the judge reread the felony-murder charge. After the jury filed out, Kunstler stated that he had a speaking engagement that evening, and requested that the night's deliberations end at 9:30 P.M. The judge said that he would consider it, and the long wait continued.

Back in my office we sat watching a show on a small portable television that a friend had brought down. I could not concentrate on the program. Conversation became desultory. Pat Skagen continued to smoke.

At 9:45 P.M. we were called back to the courtroom. There had been no note; Justice Warner had decided to suspend deliberations for the night. The jury was brought down, but it turned out that their intentions were entirely different from those of the judge.

THE COURT: Members of the jury, it is now 9:45, and you've been at it now since approximately a quarter to ten this morning . . . Therefore I'm going to suspend your deliberations until tomorrow morning at ten o'clock . . .

Suddenly the jury's foreman rose and spoke up:

Your Honor . . . I wonder if it would be possible for us to deliberate for one more hour. We were just about to take a vote on a very important point, and we [have] moved quite rapidly in the last hour. I think it would be very valuable for us.

THE COURT: Let me say to you, Mr. Foreman and members of the jury, we are not concerned here with speed. We're concerned with deliberations. Now if you feel that you might be able to accomplish your purpose in an hour, that's one thing, but I don't want you to feel that speed is of the essence. Do you understand?

THE FOREMAN: Yes.

Justice Warner called Kunstler and me up to the bench for a conference outside the hearing of the jury.

Kunstler was not happy with this turn of events, but he had no choice; he would cancel his speaking engagement. I said, "Your Honor, I think the very fact that the foreman made [this] statement is . . . a clear indication of their desire to continue, and I think it would be very sad to destroy [their] train of thought . . ." Justice Warner agreed, and sent the jury back upstairs. Before doing so, however, he again warned them that time was of no consequence, and that they need not limit themselves to one hour if they needed more.

At that moment we were so near a murder verdict that it was palpable. Gone from my mind were all thoughts save those of complete victory. All the signs indicated this. While approaching the jury box, the jurors had all been bunched together, and the male jurors had politely stood aside to let the women take their seats. They were well-disposed toward one another. It was not a jury hopelessly divided by personal animosity. They were on the verge of a conviction—at least, so I thought.

We hung around the courtroom. Everyone felt that the end might come at any moment. Slumped in a seat in the back, Kunstler looked tired and worried. Looking at him, I wondered in how many courtrooms across the land William M. Kunstler had sat slumped, tired and worried. I could not help feeling a certain admiration for the man. But the mood passed quickly. Kunstler did not really matter, and neither did I. Once the trial ended, we would go our separate ways, each of us to prosper in his own fashion.

Pat Skagen did matter, and by now she was strung tighter than a bowstring. James Richardson mattered, too, but from his appearance one could not tell what he was feeling.

At 10:40 P.M. another note came down: "The jury requests that at this time it be escorted to the hotel."

This indicated that the jurors had not been able to agree upon the murder count. It meant that deadlock, compromise or acquittal were likely. It also meant another sleepless night.

At noon the next day the following note came down: "The jury requests model of the subway station and all photographs as placed into evidence."

These materials were sent upstairs, and shortly thereafter another note came down: "Please read count number one as per charge to the jury. *Please read slowly.* The jury also requests the reading of count number two."

Again the jurors appeared in the courtroom. They were tired and haggard; it was obvious that they were under strain and that they had been working hard. The judge read the two counts to them in a firm, slow voice. Never in my life had I seen twelve people listen to anything more intently. After hearing the murder and the manslaughter charges, they returned upstairs.

Back in my office, we were beyond conversation; we simply sat and waited in silence while the hours dragged by. I was still wearing the same suit. Pat Skagen was still smoking.

The next note came at 4:25 P.M.: "Please read count number two and count number three as per charge to the jury. Please read slowly for better comprehension of all jurors. Thank you."

I read this with a sick feeling. To me it meant that the jury had rejected the murder charge and were working their way down to acquittal. The charges were read slowly.

At 6:10 P.M. we broke again for dinner. Nobody had an appetite.

At 8:30 P.M. I was summoned back to the courtroom. Another note, I thought, but as soon as I entered I knew that there had been a verdict. The tension in the room was electric. I looked at Morris Krohn. Without a word, he nodded his head. It was almost over.

I took my place at the prosecutor's table, and Kunstler and Richardson sat at the counsel table. The courtroom was practically empty: Pat Skagen sat in the second row with the detectives, and a handful of Richardson's friends were present. Kunstler's assistant had put down her knitting.

Justice Warner entered and spoke to us: "Before the jury enters the courtroom, let me state that no one is to leave the courtroom until the jury has left." The jurors filed in, grim and tired. My heart was pounding furiously. As always with verdicts, it was a moment of high drama.

Morris Krohn played out his role: "All jurors are now present, your Honor. Mr. Foreman, will you please rise?" The foreman rose. "Have the jury agreed upon a verdict?"

"Yes."

Kunstler and Richardson rose.

COURT CLERK KROHN: As to the first count of the indictment, charging the defendant with the crime of felony murder, how do you find the defendant, guilty or not guilty?

FOREMAN: Not guilty.

COURT CLERK KROHN: As to the second count of the indictment, manslaughter in the second degree, how do you find the defendant, guilty or not guilty?

FOREMAN: Guilty.

COURT CLERK KROHN: As to the third count of the indictment, charging the defendant with the crime of attempted murder, how do you find the defendant, guilty or not guilty?

FOREMAN: Not guilty.

COURT CLERK KROHN: As to the fourth count of the indictment, charging the defendant with the crime of escape in the second degree, how do you find the defendant, guilty or not guilty?

FOREMAN: Not guilty.

COURT CLERK KROHN: As to the fifth count of the indictment, charging the defendant with the crime of possessing a weapon as a felony, how do you find the defendant, guilty or not guilty?

FOREMAN: Guilty.

COURT CLERK KROHN: As to the sixth count of the indictment, charging the defendant with the crime of reckless endangerment in the second degree, how do you find the defendant, guilty or not guilty?

FOREMAN: Not guilty.

COURT CLERK KROHN: As to the seventh count of the indictment, charging the defendant with the crime of criminal possession of stolen property in the third degree, how do you find the defendant, guilty or not guilty?

FOREMAN: Guilty.

30

Pat Skagen

I sat stunned, not knowing what to feel. After hearing that first "Not guilty," it took a few seconds to realize that the jury had convicted James Richardson of Manslaughter in the Second Degree. I felt no elation, only a numb, letdown feeling. The jury had also decided that James Richardson had possessed a gun and a stolen badge; the rest they had rejected.

It was a compromise verdict. The jury had found James Richardson guilty of recklessly killing John Skagen, but not of murdering him. In their minds he was not *that* guilty.

On its face, the pattern of three convictions and four acquittals seemed inconsistent; but later, when I reflected on the overall verdict, I came to see a logic to it. The murder and the escape charge, for instance, had been closely related to one another in both my summation and the judge's charge. Once the jury had decided to reject murder and opt for the lesser homicide charge, consistency would require a rejection of the escape charge. Otherwise the escape combined with the manslaughter convictions would have revealed that they really believed that Richardson had committed a felony murder. Similarly, I could see the attempted murder count falling for the simple reason that Skagen had died, and after convicting Richardson for a successful killing, an "attempt" conviction would appear superfluous and even vindictive. The reckless endangerment had always been a relatively minor misdemeanor which no one had paid much attention to during the trial. It was keyed to the interchange between Jacobsen and Richardson rather than the primary confrontation between Skagen, Wieber and Richardson, and as such it was lost in the shuffle. The gun, possession and the stolen property charges were closely tied to the primary confrontation, and had been overwhelmingly proved. They led to convictions.

Looking stricken, Kunstler asked that the jury be polled. One by one, Morris Krohn asked each member to rise and affirm the verdict announced by the foreman. Young and middle-aged, male and female, black, white and Hispanic, each juror rose and confirmed it with conviction.

Then Justice Warner turned to the jury and addressed them for the last time. He thanked them for their services, and told them that they had performed perhaps the most serious and difficult obligation that can befall a citizen of these United States, and had performed it well. Though the judge's words were part of a routine speech that is given to all juries, in this case they seemed particularly true. When he was done, the judge nodded his head and the jurors silently filed from the courtroom and were gone.

We watched them leave. The people of Bronx County had spoken, and what remained was for the professionals, for Justice Warner, myself and William Kunstler. I turned to the judge. There was one piece of business left, for which I had little stomach. I asked that James Richardson be remanded to the Bronx House of Detention until he was sentenced. He was now a convicted felon, I pointed out, found guilty by a jury of his peers of taking a human life. The presumption of innocence had been overcome, and the temptation to flee before the date of sentence would be great. I acknowledged that it was not mandatory that the defendant be remanded, but asked that it be done. Sooner or later James Richardson would go to jail, and I felt that there was no point in putting the moment off.

Kunstler replied with heat that there was no good reason for locking up his client now. Richardson had never once failed to appear at a calendar call or trial date in this case; he was a productive citizen gainfully employed and without a pre-sentence report; and it was premature to incarcerate him.

Justice Warner asked for the particulars of Richardson's employment, and after conferring briefly with his client Kunstler offered additional details. Richardson was supporting five children. Under the judge's questioning, it developed that he was living with another woman, but that he sent money to the children, who lived with his wife. The amount of support he provided was never stated, but it was a voluntary act, not in response to a separation agreement or court order.

Through all of this Richardson was silent. Nothing, not even the announcement of conviction, broke his reserve.

Justice Warner hesitated a few minutes, stared hard at Richardson, and then ruled. Bail would be continued; the defendant would remain free until the day of sentence. Court was adjourned.

This last was too much for Pat Skagen. When she saw Richardson, freshly convicted of killing her husband, leaving the courtroom surrounded by friends, still a free man, she lost control. Looking as if she was ready to kill, she screamed, "You son of a bitch!" Dom Cuccio and Richie Gest hurried her out of the courtroom.

When I returned to my office, Pat Skagen was there alone, crying. Gone was the iron resolve and tension of all the long weeks of trial; at long last she was letting her emotions out. I let her cry.

After a time she looked up, wiped her eyes and began to talk. "Why did he do that? That black bastard should be in jail. He killed my husband and made my little boy an orphan. And did you hear that he left his own kids without a father and ran off with another woman! Why did the judge let him go? I don't understand."

She started to cry again. All the hurt and loss was written on her face. "You know that night in the hospital while Jack was dying? A neighbor watched the baby, and I went down there. No one would tell me what had happened. I stood in the hall outside the operating room and no one would speak to me. And then I saw those bums who work with Richardson—you know, the ones who were at the trial. They were in the hallway, and I heard one of them saying to another, 'Hey, guess what, Jimmy Richardson just iced a pig!'

"That's when I knew that Jack was dead. Those bastards! You know, Jack and I had decided to have another child. It would have been our second. Richardson's kids have got each other. Who will my son have?"

So, in a sense, there had been two deaths in the case, not one. There was nothing that I could say to Pat Skagen. But I tried, and after a while she calmed down. I asked Richie Gest to take her home, and then I, too, went home and slept.

31

Sentence

The weeks sped by. My "victory" had been celebrated briefly by people around the courthouse, and then was forgotten. There were new trials, new crimes, new lawyers, and it wasn't long before everyone had turned his attention elsewhere.

After the verdict, the cast of the trial dispersed. The detectives were all "back on the chart," catching new cases. Pat Skagen was at home with John Jr.; James Richardson was working the night shift at the hospital; Kunstler was in Buffalo defending an Attica inmate accused of murdering a prison guard; and Justice Warner was presiding over another murder trial.

I had no time to relax, either. My caseload had been neglected over the weeks, and defense attorneys were literally lined up outside my door demanding trials for their clients. I tried to oblige, and within two weeks I was back in court.

It was only occasionally that I found time to give thought to the question of Richardson's sentence. It concerned me only indirectly, and in the final analysis would be answered by Justice Warner. Both in law and in fact, he alone had the power to impose sentence, and in this particular case his latitude would be immense. On a Manslaughter 2 conviction, he could give Richardson anything from a suspended sentence to fifteen years. I did not have the faintest idea what he would do, but if there was one thing that I had learned about Ivan Warner during the long weeks of trial, it was that he was a strong-minded and independent judge who would make up his own mind on this question. I did not believe that anything I might say at the time of sentence would be likely to have a significant impact on his decision.

Still, as the date of sentencing drew near, I gave more and more thought to my recommendation. What motivated me was a personal desire to articulate once and for all some of my thoughts about sentencing and punishment. I had devoted many months of my life to sending James Richardson to jail, and it seemed to me that I had an obligation to state, publicly and on the record, why I felt that he belonged there.

The more I thought about it, the more difficult it was to crystallize my thoughts. I was torn by the same ambivalence that had troubled me months earlier when I had attempted to negotiate a plea. I could not seem to translate a complex, emotion-laden tragedy into a number. However harsh or lenient, no sentence would undo what had been done, and no words spoken at the time of sentencing could adequately express all that needed to be said.

After the verdict, I never discussed the question of Richardson's sentence with anyone in either the district attorney's office or the Police Department. At the time of sentencing, consistent with his conspiratorial view of the universe, Kuntsler would accuse me of speaking as a "puppet of the establishment." It was not so. My words at that time were my own, poor and inadequate though they proved to be. The only person with whom I talked about the problem was my wife, and we sat up late struggling with our conflicting emotions. I was concerned that both the partisan role I had taken during the trial and the anger I felt at some of the things Kunstler had said during his summation might have affected my objectivity.

James Richardson was sentenced on Friday, December 13, 1974. It was like a reunion; after seven weeks, everyone was back for the final act of the drama. Pat Skagen, the detectives, the crew from Lincoln Hospital, the buffs, Kunstler, Richardson, Morris Krohn and I were all in our accustomed places in a packed courtroom. Only the jury was missing.

When Justice Warner entered the room we all rose.

Justice Warner: "Arraign the defendant for sentence."

The Clerk: "Yes, your Honor. Mr. James Richardson, is that your name, sir?"

At last James Richardson spoke. His voice was soft. "Yes."

The Clerk: "Is the gentleman standing to your left Mr. William Kunstler, your attorney?"

"Yes, he is."

Following the sentencing ritual Morris Krohn turned to me and asked whether I had a statement to make.

Even in those last few moments, as I looked around the courtroom—first at Pat Skagen, then at Kunstler and Richardson—I was not sure of precisely what I would say, and when I rose to speak, my words were unrehearsed.

I had long agonized over this moment, I told the court, and felt that I did have to make a recommendation. Then I stated that I did not believe that prison would either reform or rehabilitate James Richardson, and that in this sense no useful purpose would be served by incarcerating him. Further, I admitted that sending Richardson to jail would not serve to deter others from committing similar crimes. Finally, I acknowledged that although I did not consider James Richardson a good man, as Kunstler did, he certainly was not among the worst I had ever been called upon to prosecute.

Having said all this, I stated why I felt Richardson should

be sent to jail. I alluded briefly to his past criminal record, and then turned to the facts of this case:

> . . . James Richardson was walking the streets of the Bronx armed with a pistol, and . . . he had no right to be so armed . . . he is not what is commonly thought of [as] a cop killer . . . but the fact remains that he shot down a police officer . . . [and] caused unbelievable and crushing tragedy to that officer's family . . . he also dealt a terrible blow to the . . . fabric that holds society together . . . I submit to your Honor that this case requires . . . that there be punishment precisely because the defendant in his actions on that day dealt this blow . . . recklessly. He had no business with a gun. He had no business drawing on a police officer and firing those four shots. I submit . . . that the defendant's actions have become important . . . in an arena that . . . transcends the defendant's own person . . . Justice is not only meted out to the defendant, but to the society in which he finds himself . . . [to] the . . . people in this county who don't walk around with guns . . . who do not [commit] reckless and violent acts . . . the overwhelming majority of people who rely upon the police and have left in the policeman's hands the duty of protecting the public . . . That society is entitled . . . to know that a man who draws recklessly on a police officer and fires . . . is punished. That society is entitled to know that [it] can be made safe from such people . . . because of that . . . I am recommending to this Court that a sentence of a five-year minimum and a fifteen-year maximum be imposed.

I sat down, and Morris Krohn then turned to the defense table and asked, "Mr. Kunstler, do you wish to say anything?"

Not surprisingly, Kunstler either refused or was unable to understand the ambiguities that I was wrestling with. For him, the case was as simple as black and white, and in my words he heard nothing but hypocrisy and dishonesty. But sentencing is a more serious affair than the animosity between attorneys, and soon he turned his attention to matters more relevant than his opinion of the prosecution. He spoke of Richardson the man, and of the waste of sending such a man to jail. He spoke

eloquently, echoing my very words uttered minutes earlier: "
. . . to send [Richardson] to jail serves what purpose? . . . To
reform him? To rehabilitate him? He doesn't need rehabilitation, Judge. He is working for the City of New York . . . What
possible gain to society can there be by sending him to jail?"

Then at last Kunstler got around to saying what I would
have said had I been in his shoes. He indicted a society that
is ready to imprison its poor and its black for their crimes, while
turning its back on the equally serious crimes of the wealthy
and powerful. He put the case in the perspective of Watergate
and the Vietnam war, and there was truth in what he said:

> Judge, too many people are going to jail, and we are creating
> . . . a society of recidivists . . . They go to Attica or some other
> place, and come back, and then you have the end of a human
> being . . . [How] are you going to explain to society why Richard
> Kliendienst, the highest law-enforcement official in the land,
> pleads guilty to perjury in the performance of his duties and
> walks out with a hundred-dollar fine. Or why the President of the
> United States, guilty of the most grievous crimes, is pardoned,
> or why . . . Mr. Agnew walks the streets . . . Then you take this
> crazy, grotesque incident . . . To put [Richardson] in jail is just
> to create another human tragedy . . . We know . . . that it is
> usually the black and Puerto Rican and poor who get the maxi-
> mum sentences . . . and that it is white men and women who
> are corrupting our society . . .

Kunstler went on and on, becoming repetitious in his
denunciations of such matters as the Nixon pardon, and then
abruptly he sat down.

Morris Krohn asked the defendant whether he wished to
speak in his own behalf before sentence was imposed. Richardson said, "No, I don't."

The time had come for the judge to speak:

At the outset, let me make . . . myself perfectly clear. Whatever
sentence I will impose here this afternoon, I want it understood by
everyone that such sentence will not be imposed because the victim

involved in this instance was a police officer. Let's have that clearly understood.

True, I as a judge of this Court am concerned with the wellbeing of police officers, but I am just as much concerned with the wellbeing and safety of all of the eight million people in the City of New York . . .

This defendant, James Richardson, thirty-one years of age . . . was indicted by the Grand Jury, charged with the crime of murder, manslaughter in the second degree, attempted murder, escape in the second degree, possession of a weapon as a felony, reckless endangerment and criminal possession of stolen property.

The jury, after deliberating for . . . several days, returned a verdict of guilty as to manslaughter in the second degree, possession of a weapon as a felony and criminal possession of stolen property. [The defendant] has had two prior violations with the law: one in Monroe County in this state where he received three years probation, [and] another . . . in Kings County, which appears to have been dismissed . . .

This case [is] one of the most bizarre, unusual situations I believe that this Court will ever be confronted with. However, the fact remains that an individual . . . is dead.

The defendant, Mr. Richardson, appears to have been raised in a good home, both parents working people, and he himself [is] presently employed at Lincoln Hospital . . . as a senior admitting clerk. And although he is not living with his wife and family, there is indication that he does make weekly payments. There is no evidence of any use of drugs on his part. It appears that for some years now he has made every effort to conduct himself as a law-abiding citizen. However, a law-abiding citizen . . . does not arm himself with a loaded revolver. It didn't have to be Officer Skagen in that subway. It could have been a civilian, and the very same thing could have happened because James Richardson took it upon himself to arm himself with a loaded .32 caliber gun. So I think we are making too much of this police officer business . . . We have to begin someplace to make the community safe for everybody, and until we do that, it is going to be safe for nobody.

I have come to the strong belief—and I believe that any rational and reasonable person would also come to the same conclusion—that these United States of ours at the present time can clearly be considered the number one murder capital of the world. I don't believe that anywhere in this world is a life looked upon so cheaply . . . Murders are committed daily without rhyme or reason . . . Possibly the time has come for us to give serious consideration to an arms-limitation agreement for [our] various communities . . . rather than attempting to have an arms-limitation agreement for the world.

This case presents . . . a clear picture of the senseless killing with which we are daily confronted. It is clear evidence of the depravity of human nature and the depth to which we have fallen. We all carry . . . too much hate in our hearts and minds, and hate is nothing but murder on the way . . .

Now, while Mr. Richardson may not have fired the shots that proved fatal to Mr. Skagen, he did shoot the officer, did run upstairs, criminally deceiving uniformed policemen . . . We may never know, and we should not speculate, as to what started the altercation on the subway platform but we do know that . . . a life was brutally snuffed out . . .

As far as the police officer, Wieber, is concerned . . . I believe that serious consideration should be given to the question of whether our police officers are adequately prepared for their jobs . . . Should there be periodic stringent examinations to assure that the officer maintains himself in such condition as to fully protect himself and the public, particularly in his handling of his revolver? It seems to me . . . that where we have a police officer to whom we have given the right to carry a revolver to protect us, we should make sure that he can operate that revolver to the . . . best of his ability.

Punishment is in itself an evil, and it can be justified only as a means of attaining a greater good. To suffer punishment is to pay a debt . . . Justice requires that the debt be paid and the wrong satisfied . . . This Court has studied hard and long regarding the sentence to impose this afternoon . . . and I believe that . . . to sentence Mr. Richardson to anything less than total confinement for some period of time would unduly depreciate the seriousness of the offense . . .

James Richardson, it is the sentence of this Court that upon your conviction for the crime of manslaughter in the second degree you be committed to the custody of the State Department of Corrections for a term not to exceed ten years; that upon your conviction of the crime of possession of a weapon as a felony you be committed . . . for a term not to exceed seven years; and that upon your conviction for the crime of criminal possession of stolen property in the third degree as a misdemeanor you are unconditionally discharged. All sentences are to run concurrent.

THE CLERK: James Richardson, you have a right to appeal. You must exercise this right within thirty days. If you are without funds, the Appellate Division will give you counsel and order a transcript of the minutes. Do you understand this?

DEFENDANT RICHARDSON: Yes.

THE CLERK: Mr. Kunstler, will you remain with your client for thirty days on his rights to appeal?

MR. KUNSTLER: Yes . . .

32

Aftermath

James Richardson did not go to jail on the day he was sentenced. Instead, Kunstler applied for and obtained a stay of judgment, and Richardson remained out on bail pending the outcome of his appeal. I opposed this application and lost, but in the process I extracted a promise from Kunstler before the court that he would not delay in preparing and filing his appellate briefs. This promise was not kept.

But though he did not go to jail, Richardson did lose his job at Lincoln Hospital. He was indefinitely suspended without pay, and shortly after the trial he went on welfare for the first time in his life. He was not alone on the unemployment rolls. Deepening recession and a generation of gross municipal mismanagement would take their toll on New York City. Within a year over two thousand police officers and tens of thousands of other municipal employees had been laid off in a desperate effort to balance the city's budget. Had he lived, John Skagen would probably have been among them.

* * *

It was almost a year before a brief was submitted on Richardson's behalf to the Appellate Division of the State Supreme Court. Listed as counsel on the brief were Kunstler and Roseann Kaplan, a recent law-school graduate.

I did not handle the appeal of the Richardson case for the district attorney's office. I would have liked to do so, but by that time I was enmeshed in an investigation concerning the death of a Puerto Rican drug addict who had been beaten by police officers while in a precinct jail cell. Ultimately I obtained indictments against a number of police officers for murder, assault, and perjury. I simply could not take time off from this investigation to prepare the Richardson brief.

So the appeal was assigned to Jane Koch, a senior assistant in the Appeals Bureau. We discussed the case at some length, and I turned over to her my files, but in the end she had no choice except to undertake the arduous task of absorbing the transcripts in their entirety. It took her several months to prepare a brief, which, when concluded, ran seventy-three printed pages. It was a good brief, and persuasively replied to the issues raised by the defense.

The appeal was argued before five justices of the Appellate Division on March 30, 1976, some fifteen months after Richardson had been sentenced. Jane Koch argued for the district attorney's office, and Roseann Kaplan for the defendant. Kunstler was in Connecticut trying another murder case, but James Richardson and a number of his friends attended. I, too, sat in the audience.

From the very outset of the oral argument it became clear that only one issue was bothering the judges. They gave short shrift to the defense claims that Richardson had been denied a fair trial either in the jury selection process or in my summation, and rejected the assertion that his confessions had been improperly placed in evidence. Instead, the argument, which lasted almost an hour, revolved entirely around the question of the legal sufficiency of the evidence behind the manslaughter conviction. More specifically, the judges wondered aloud whether the evidence established beyond a reasonable doubt that Richardson's direct actions caused the death of John Skagen. Justice Warner's refusal to charge the jury with my theory of Richardson's vicarious responsibility for Wieber's bullets had removed that theory from the case. Since the jury had not heard this reasoning from the judge it was assumed that they had not considered it in arriving at their verdict, and so had relied upon the traditional direct-causation standard that they had been given.

In the final analysis, it all seemed to boil down to a single question: Did the shoulder wounds directly inflicted by Richardson contribute to Skagen's death? The medical examiner had answered yes, but had qualified his answer, stating that the major damage had been done by the police bullets. Dr. Spain, the defense expert, had flatly asserted that the shoulder wounds were insignificant and had nothing whatsoever to do with the cause of death.

By its verdict, the jury implicitly indicated that it believed the medical examiner, not Dr. Spain. Jane Koch argued that the jury's factual determination in resolving the conflicting testimony should not be overturned, and that the appellate court should not exercise its discretion in substituting its judgment for that of the trier of the facts. As the argument went on, it became clear to me that the judges were troubled by the manslaughter conviction, and were not persuaded that causation had been adequately proved. When they retired to deliberate, I had forebodings that the conviction would not be sustained.

On April 13, 1976, the Appellate Division unanimously reversed the manslaughter conviction, holding as a matter of fact and law that the causal link between Richardson's recklessness and Skagen's death had not been established. It unanimously affirmed the felony-gun and the stolen-property conviction, and rejected the claim that Richardson had been denied a fair trial. The case was remanded to Justice Warner for resentencing on the weapons charge.

On the same day that the Richardson appeal was argued, Lincoln Hospital was shut down and replaced by a new $200 million facility bearing the same name. Physically, it is a vast improvement over its predecessor, and hopes are high that the quality of medical care in the South Bronx will improve. But the odds are against it, and the challenges that face the new hospital are just as awesome as those that destroyed its predecessor. In any event, the Lincoln Hospital where John Skagen died and James Richardson worked is no more. It, too, was a victim.

Dr. Richard Taft, the defense witness who worked at Lincoln Hospital, also became a victim. He was found dead one morning several months after the trial, lying on the floor of a hospital supply closet, a hypodermic syringe stuck in his forearm. Apparently he had overdosed on heroin.

William Kunstler went up to Buffalo, New York, to try the first Attica case, which was another well-publicized extravaganza, much more his kind of political trial than the Richardson case had been. As in the Bronx case, the charge in Buffalo was murder. He had a dead body to contend with rather than one of those bloodless, victimless, hard-to-understand conspiratorial indictments that had figured so heavily in his celebrated past victories. Kunstler "lost" in Buffalo—which is to say that a jury convicted his client of murder. In a narrow, factual sense, there is no reason to imagine that the verdict was unjust.

In a larger sense, it soon became clear that it was not Kunstler personally but society itself that lost terribly in the Attica prosecutions. A federal agent admitted that Kunstler's entourage had been secretly infiltrated and spied upon during the pre-trial period. More important, a special assistant attorney general working on the prosecution team for the State of New York quit, making the scathing charge that his superiors had deliberately mishandled the investigation so that only Attica inmates would be prosecuted, while the equally or even more guilty law enforcement hierarchy would be exonerated. Eventually investigation would reveal that this charge was fundamentally correct.

Attica is another story, and one that has been well told by others. For Kunstler it was merely another episode in an unfolding saga, another opportunity for him to be both wrong and right, to be both obnoxious and endearing, to be both painfully truthful and shamelessly demagogic. Viewed from afar, he seemed to me to be replaying on a larger stage his role in the Richardson case.

From time to time, George Wieber has stopped by my office for a chat. He has a child now, a fat, healthy baby boy, and a second is on the way. He is still at the 41st Precinct, and is still working with John Jacobsen.

Jake, who had lost his wife in a tragic automobile accident, has remarried; George tells me that the kids have taken to their new mother, and that it is wonderful to see them together.

For Wieber and Jacobsen, June 28, 1972, is a long time ago, and they never discuss it.

About a year after the trial ended, Al the Opera Singer died. He has been missed around the courthouse.

I visited Pat Skagen recently. She has not remarried, and lives alone with her son in a modest attached house in a quiet Bronx neighborhood. The boy is in grade school, and raising him has been a full-time job for her. She is doing it well.

Pat Skagen seems to be at peace with herself. She is far more relaxed than she was during the tension-filled days of the trial. I told her of the appeal and asked her what she thought.

"You know," she said, "as I look back on it, I don't hate Richardson anymore. I feel sorry for him. He was kind of pitiful —pathetic, really—sitting there throughout the trial. I really can't hate him."

"John Jr. once asked me about Richardson," she went on, "and I told him that he was not a bad man, but a man who did a bad thing. I told him that because I don't want him to grow up with hatred. In the world in which he is growing up, he cannot afford to hate."

It took me another year to realize that I had to leave the district attorney's office. It was a good year for me—too good a year. The Richardson "victory" was followed by others, and these produced a bit of publicity and the beginnings of a reputation as a prosecutor. I had become a seasoned professional, and at last I found that I was at home with both the cops and the robbers in the netherworld of the South Bronx. I had matured as a prosecutor, and I loved the investigations and the trials.

That was the problem. No one should be permitted to make a lifetime career out of prosecuting his fellow man. Over the years the investigations and trials cannot help but create a warped, pessimistic and self-righteous attitude toward humanity. Just as a woman who teaches kindergarten may in time unconsciously treat all the people she meets as if they were children, so do most veteran prosecutors, after years of viewing the world through a sewer of violence and depravity, unconsciously come to divide humanity into helpless victims and vicious perpetrators. It is an ugly and unfair view. Worse still is the arrogance that comes from wielding power too long. Good prosecution requires self-confidence and the ability to make painful and difficult decisions, but in the long run the decisions stop being difficult, and the self-confidence becomes arrogance and self-righteousness.

I could sense the seeds of these qualities in myself, and I

could see them full-blown in many of the career prosecutors I knew. The time had come to get out. It was not easy to quit; it never is, to leave something that has become familiar, comfortable and successful. I was truly sad when I resigned my appointment.

So this is a time of changes for me, of new problems, challenges and uncertainties. For the time being—or perhaps forever—the world of criminal justice is behind me. But in another sense it will always be with me, for there is no end to the James Richardson case or to any of the others—only new beginnings.

On May 27, 1976, James Richardson was resentenced to three years in state prison.

About the Author

STEVEN PHILLIPS was born in New York City and educated at Williams College and Columbia Law School. In 1971 he joined the staff of the district attorney of Bronx County. Between 1973 and 1975 he successfully prosecuted more than a dozen murder cases, and appeared several times before the highest appellate courts in New York State. Currently he is associated with Kreindler & Kreindler, a leading New York civil-litigation firm.

Mr. Phillips lives in New York City with his wife and daughter.